DEMONIC CONSPIRACY KNOWN AS CALVINISM

The truth about Calvinism no one else
has had the insight or courage to reveal!

Ron Craig

Pastor of

Living Way Fellowship

ISBN: 978-1-63945-249-1 (Paperback)
       978-1-63945-265-1 (Hardback)
       978-1-63945-266-8 (Ebook)

Writers' Branding
1800-608-6550
www.writersbranding.com
orders@writersbranding.com

In this book, all Scripture passages are quoted from the King James Bible Version—though some words are updated for a better understanding. [Bracketed words] within quotations from either God's Holy Word or John Calvin's written works are this author's explanation of the words before or after those brackets. Within quotes from Scripture, and John Calvin's written works, lower case words which are in *italics*, as well as the words in *ALL CAPITALS* (also in *italics*), are the emphases of this author. And certain words by this author are in *italics* or *ALL CAPITALS*. The quotes from both Scripture and John Calvin's works are from the WORDsearch digital library, and are used by permission. Works other than Scripture are John Calvin's "Institutes of the Christian Religion" and his Bible Commentaries. *You can access even more books by this author on our church website—* www.livingwayfellowshiponline.org. Thanks for visiting us online!

Contents

Acknowledgments

I acknowledge first of all my Lord and Savior, Jesus Christ—Who has given me all the revelation contained within this volume. I also thank my wife, Joan, and all of the other members of *LIVING WAY FELLOWSHIP* for their patience and support of me in all of my authoring endeavors. And, I pray that this book, as well as all my other publications, will honor each of them.

Introduction

Because of the *TITLE* of this book there ought to be *NO* misunderstanding about the material it deals with: *CALVINISM is obviously the subject of this unique work. But, TAGING CALVINISM AS A DEMONIC CONSPIRACY might seem to some as being a little TOO SEVERE.* After all—*five hundred years of ACCEPTANCE by multitudes around the planet is likely considered an indication that CALVINISM IS EITHER A GENUINE ALTERNATIVE VIEW of Scripture, or the actual CORRECT INTERPRETATION of Scripture.* (And the devil just *SMILES* over that!)

While searching to find out if another book existed with this same title—even though I found none—in the process I did discover numerous books that contained within them the term—Calvinist Conspiracy. Several of those books used that very terminology to demonstrate how different religious and political groups, in different nations, and in different centuries, have achieved their different religious and political goals. My motivation for penning this volume, however, is *NEITHER RELIGIOUS NOR POLITICAL*; but rather to scripturally demonstrate that *John Calvin's doctrinal system is totally deceptive; and that through his written works, his HERESIES have been ENTRENCHED IN CHURCHES WORLDWIDE; and have caused untold damage to untold numbers of BOTH believers and non-believers alike. I will also fill the void resulting from the elimination of Calvinist falsehoods— which multitudes over five centuries HAVE TRUSTED IN for their salvation—with actual SAVING Bible Truth.*

Somebody once asked me: "How much of Calvinism is *TRUE?*" My answer: *"ZERO!"* Am I suggesting there is no truth in any of John Calvin's written works? When Calvin quoted Scripture, he was obviously quoting the truth. But, Calvin *QUOTING* God's Word did not *MAKE* God's Word the truth. Holy Scripture *IS* the truth! *One of Calvin's big errors was his deliberate distortion of the Scriptures he quoted.* Calvin would either *ADD TO* what some Bible verses actually say, *TAKE AWAY FROM* the clear message of other passages, or deliberately *ALTER* the meaning of some words in those passages—making his end-product totally different from the original. The Bible repeatedly condemns such practice by anybody—including preachers. Therefore, *it cannot be that Christ approves of John Calvin's deceptive, demonic theology.*

Of the many truths I emphasize in this work, at the *TOP* of the list—Multitudes of people are *NEGATIVELY AFFECTED* by Calvin's *DEMONIC* falsehoods, although they have *NEVER HEARD* of John Calvin—while others have heard of him, but would *NOT* consider themselves Calvinists. Calvin's errors go *FAR* beyond his teachings on Predestination and the Elect. In the voices of *MANY* believers today I constantly hear the echo of Calvinism in one form or another. And it is all ultra-unbiblical!

ONE Scripture passage is all it takes to completely destroy Calvin's *ENTIRE* theological system. *Just one! I do not mean that ONLY ONE Scripture EXISTS that does so, but that IT REQUIRES ONLY ONE TO DO SO. One of the EMBARRASSING facts about that fact is that MANY passages that destroy Calvinism have been in the Bible all along!* But, *preachers have either COWARDLY failed to expose Calvin's errors—or actually JOINED Calvin in disseminating those errors! Whatever contradicts God's Word is demonic* (1 Timothy 4:1). *Calvinism is demonic!*

Chapter I

John Calvin's brazen dishonesty

I will first lay out the *BASICS* of Calvinism in simple form. *ALL* of Calvin's theological errors sprang from his *MISUNDERSTANDING OF GOD'S SOVEREIGNTY. Calvin was convinced that God being Sovereign means that He orchestrates everything that happens in heaven and on earth—both good and bad.* Otherwise, *God might not be considered Sovereign, His Glory might be tarnished and He might no longer be respected.* Thus, *John Calvin felt obligated to PROTECT both the Sovereignty and Glory of God BY his theology. And that assumption exposed still another FLAW in Calvin's theology—thinking that God's Glory and Sovereignty both needed protection—and that by man.* But, *if God is God, He can protect Himself!*

Moreover, if everything which happens does happen because God has *PREPLANNED* it to happen, *then God is behind THEOLOGICAL ERROR as well as Bible Truth! In every way, Calvinism is EXPOSED as unbiblical and ridiculous*—if we examine it by the Word of God, rather than by human speculation. This book does just that!

Like philosophers, Calvin tried to explain worldwide evil. But unlike philosophers, *John Calvin attempted to explain it by Scripture.* But, in his attempts, he actually massacred the Scriptures. The church would be better off today had John Calvin had a *DIFFERENT CAREER.* As disrespectful as that may sound, what about all the *DAMAGE* Calvin has done to the church and the Bible; and to God's reputation? Instead of being a *BLESSING,* Calvinism has given the devil a *TOOL* against both God and His people. John Calvin was a villain—not a hero!

God being Sovereign (based upon *CALVIN'S VIEW* of Sovereignty), *and evil prevailing on this earth, that had to mean that God Himself is somehow the CAUSE of all evil as well as all good*—John Calvin's theology. *Yet we dare not accuse the Creator of WRONGDOING*—Calvin's theology—*although Adam's fall was preplanned BY his very OWN Creator*—John Calvin's theology. *God carried out that plan against Adam by sending the devil to the Garden of Eden to TEMPT Adam and Eve to SIN*—again, Calvin's theology. *God withheld His Grace from the two, so Adam and Eve could not keep from sinning*—Calvin's theology. Yet *ADAM'S FALL WAS ADAM'S FAULT*—once again, Calvin's theology. *THOSE DEMONIC DOCTRINES ARE SCATTERED THROUGHOUT* Calvin's "Institutes of the Christian Religion" and his Bible Commentaries.

Now, enter the most diabolical feature of Calvinism: Not only did Calvin teach that God planned Adam's fall —which *ALSO* made the entire human race a bunch of sinners—*but even claimed that, for reasons known only to God Himself, He decided to save only a small portion of fallen humanity*—the Elect—thus, purposely making redemption *OFF-LIMITS* to the majority of the *FALLEN* human race. *And John Calvin knew about all of that by his knowledge of the SECRET counsel of God—which he had discovered—even though it was SECRET!* (?????)

According to John Calvin, God had arbitrarily made His decisions regarding those individuals He wanted to save—the Elect—and those He wanted to remain lost—the Reprobate. And those Divine decisions had nothing to do with the *CHARACTER, DECISIONS* or *ACTIONS* of the Elect or the Reprobate. Instead, *GOD'S ARBITRARY WILL* was the deciding factor concerning who would be saved and who would remain lost—who would have no opportunity to be saved. *BEFORE CREATION* God made an *UNALTERABLE*

LIST OF SINNERS whom He wanted to redeem—*ALL* other sinners being the *REPROBATE—REMAINING LOST. God will PUNISH the non-elect in the Lake of Fire forever FOR HIS GLORY—even though their ELECTION TO HELL was God's decision—NOT THEIRS. And multitudes of people today believe that GARBAGE; either because they have NO knowledge of what Calvin really taught*—or they are just as hypocritical as Calvin was—either case inviting God's judgment upon them.

NONE OF THE PREVIOUS IS SPECULATION ON MY PART. Calvin's Institutes and Bible Commentaries are literally filled with those lies. *Calvinism has FIVE main points—designated by the ACROSTIC known as TULIP.* The *T* in *TULIP* means *Total Depravity*; the *U* stands for *Unconditional Election*; the *L* for *Limited Atonement*; the *I* stands for *Irresistible Grace*; the *P* for *Perseverance of the Saints—Once-Saved-Always-Saved.* Scripture *NOT ONLY BACKS NONE OF THE FIVE TULIP POINTS, BUT CATEGORICALLY REFUTES EVERY ONE OF THEM.*

One *STAUNCH* modern Calvinist, Edwin H. Palmer, admitted that each of those five *TULIP TENETS* depend upon all of the others, in order to stand. If one point is erroneous all of them are erroneous; causing the entire theological system to fall apart. Palmer was more right than he realized; *for indeed that system does fall apart; and horrendous is the doctrinal crash!*

As I stated earlier, all it takes is one Scripture to do the smashing job. However, there are numerous single passages; *each of which completely destroys Calvinism.* Now, since exposure of only one of the five points is all that is necessary for the annihilation of the entirety of Calvinism, *I NEED ONLY* address one or two of the five unbiblical points to *BLAST* them all. But, the Bible and other books I have written exposing the satanic nature of Calvinism, destroy all *FIVE* points of Calvin's *TULIP*. Calvin showed no shame in *TAMPERING* with the Word of God, in order to maintain his Demonic theology.

Calvinism has the devil's fingerprints all over it! You can begin to *SEE* that truth by Luke 19:10: Christ said that He had come into this world *TO SAVE THE LOST. Calvin claimed that God planned to save only the Elect; and abandon everyone else.* Not so Luke 19:10! Now, if Calvin had been correct, that Christ came to save only the Elect and no one else, then only the elect were lost; for Jesus said He came to save the lost. The flip side of that coin, so to speak, would mean that *ALL* the rest of humanity were *NOT LOST.* Thus, *Calvinism bit the dust by that one Scripture passage.* However, Luke 19:10 is joined by many other Bible passages that follow suit.

Romans 5:6 is yet another single Scripture passage that annihilates Calvinism. It says that Christ *DIED* for the *UNGODLY.* Well, if Christ died *ONLY* for the *ELECT,* as John Calvin taught, and Paul said that Christ *DIED* for the *UNGODLY,* then only the elect must be ungodly! *WHY* did Calvin *NOT SEE THE INCONSISTENCY* of his theology? *Because, he ALREADY had his mind made up before he consulted the Scriptures!* In order to hold onto his theology, *Calvin had to either ignore God's Word, or pervert God's Word, or somehow make it SEEM to agree with His theology.* Calvin was incompetent as a *BIBLE TEACHER,* because of his dishonesty with Bible Truth —*DISQUALIFYING him in every way*—despite his fame!

Did Adam's fall not cause EVERY human being to be lost, and therefore, *ungodly?* If so, then Christ came to save every human being! *The Gospel Truth in those two Scripture passages totally destroys Calvinism's Limited Atonement.* A couple of passages did the smashing job.

4

Therefore, no matter what John Calvin argued, *the Bible teaches that Christ died for every human being on earth.* And if one Calvinist point is false *ALL* the rest of them are false. If any of the five points is in error, then Calvin's entire theological system collapses. (*Boom!*)

In Romans 11:32, Paul stated plainly that God had confined *ALL* under disobedience—that He might have mercy on *ALL*. John Calvin claimed that God extended His mercy *ONLY* to the *ARBITRARILY elected Elect.* God deliberately withheld His mercy from all other human beings. How would Calvin handle that *CLEAR* passage, which diametrically opposed *HIS* doctrine? He claimed that—by that statement *PAUL ONLY MEANT* that those who are saved ought to ascribe their salvation to God's mercy. John Calvin literally *REWROTE* Romans 11:32, in order to make it *SEEMINGLY* back his theology. Yet, Paul said plainly that God extends mercy to the *SAME ALL*, whom He had confined to disobedience. If Calvin were correct that mercy is offered *ONLY* to God's Elect, then according to Romans 11:32, *ONLY* God's elect are disobedient. But, *ALL in Adam having a DISOBEDIENT NATURE, God's mercy is offered to ALL in Adam's race.*

One more Scripture exposing that Calvinist *LIE* is 1 Timothy 1:15, where Paul said that Christ Jesus came into the world to save sinners. One more time, if Christ shed His blood only for God's special Elect—arbitrarily chosen by God—and offered no sacrifice for *ANY* of the reprobate, because God had put them on that doomed list—then Paul's statement here would mean that only the Elect are sinners—*which would mean that all other human beings are SAINTS. I am sure you see that such reasoning is unreasonable! Obviously, everyone outside Christ is a sinner. All lost people being SINNERS, Jesus Christ obviously came into the world to SAVE ALL LOST PEOPLE.* Thus, Limited Atonement is another Calvinist falsehood—spawned by the devil himself!

The devil must revel in the atmosphere of Calvinism; because *UNDER* Calvinism's camouflage, he can do his dirty deeds without detection. The devil obviously used Calvin to *ENGINEER* Calvinism! *HONEST HANDLING* of Scripture totally destroys that demonic theology.

ALL FIVE TULIP POINTS ARE INTERCONNECTED. If one point proves *FALSE*, all the other points are *FALSE too. ALL FIVE TULIP POINTS RISE OR FALL TOGETHER. They all have to prove true, or none of them is true. And all five points are based on Calvin's ERRONEOUS view of Divine Sovereignty. Calvinism is totally ERRONEOUS!*

John Calvin taught that, before the Creator created this universe, He made *AN UNALTERABLE LIST* of who would be *ELECT,* and who would be *REPROBATE.* And since God made that list before man was created, then man has nothing to do with being one, or the other. God made that choice—and His choice cannot be overturned. *NO NAME CAN BE DELETED FROM THAT ELECT LIST! NOR* any name added to it! The Elect will be saved; and cannot ever be lost again—Perseverance of the Saints— Once-saved-always-saved. Reprobates cannot be saved *EVEN IF THEY DESPERATELY DESIRE TO GET SAVED.* Calvin's entire theology emits a demonic stench!

According to John Calvin's *INTERPRETATION* of the Bible message, Adam's fall caused Adam, and all of his offspring, to become Totally Depraved—the *T* in *TULIP.* That *MEANS* (according to Calvin) that *no human being can do anything that is worthy of God's approval.* Thus, sinners cannot even ask God to save them; *unless God first REGENERATES them so they can ask God to SAVE them.* (????) *Calvin portrayed God as A MANIPULATOR.* Moreover, *since all were SINNERS, then it would not be unjust for God to condemn them ALL to Hell—although it was GOD'S PLAN FOR ADAM TO FALL in the first place!* However, God secretly, and arbitrarily, decided to save some, while abandoning all the others to Hades. Thus, Unconditional Election is that *U* in *TULIP*. *If your name is on the Elect list, you will be saved by the Holy Spirit's secret operation.* But, *if your name is on the Reprobate list—that is too bad—NO opportunity to be saved*—John Calvin's *SHAMEFUL, BARBARIC THEOLOGY!*

Next, since God had unconditionally elected certain sinners *TO BE SAVED*, and *SOVEREIGNLY DENIED* the same opportunity to all other sinners, then it naturally followed that *Christ's blood was shed only for the Elect*: Calvin's doctrine called Limited Atonement. Why pay a redemption price for people whom God would not allow to be saved anyway? *Hence the diabolical doctrine that Christ died only for the ELECT—and no one else.* Satan was surely pleased, for that lie would discourage many from even *SEEKING* salvation! (Demonic Calvinism!)

Irresistible Grace—the *I* in *TULIP—is the sure action of the Holy Spirit in convicting Elect sinners of their sins, so they will get saved. Since they were divinely elected to be saved, then God will see to it that they get saved. The IRRESISTIBLE part of the doctrine means that they cannot possibly NOT get saved!* God the manipulator!

Even if the first four *TULIP TENETS APPEAR RIGHT, John Calvin's entire theological system would go down the tube—unless there were an assurance that the Elect will STAY SAVED*—Perseverance of the Saints—the *P* in *TULIP*—One more *Calvinist FALSEHOOD!* Because,...

John 15:6: *"If anyone ABIDES NOT in Me, he is cast out as a branch, and is withered, and the angels gather them, throw them into the FIRE, and they are burned."*

Romans 11:21-22: *"If God did not spare the natural branches* [Jews], *He may not spare you either.* Consider the goodness and severity of God—On those who *FELL,* severity—*But toward you, goodness—IF you continue in His goodness. Otherwise, YOU TOO WILL BE CUT OFF."*

Galatians 5:2-4: "If you get circumcised, *Christ will profit you nothing…You become estranged from Christ if you attempt to be justified by law—you have fallen from grace* [by which you were saved]." (Become lost again!)

Hebrews 3:6: "Christ as a Son over His own house; *whose house we* [believers] *are—IF WE HOLD FAST the confidence and the rejoicing of the hope firm to the end."* (*IF can change everything—even one's salvation status.*)

Hebrews 3:12: *"Beware BRETHREN,* lest there be in any of you an evil heart of unbelief in *DEPARTING* from God." (Depart from God—*DEPART FROM SALVATION!*)

Hebrews 3:14: "We have become partakers of Christ *IF* we hold the beginning of our confidence *STEADFAST* to the end." (What if you do not hold fast to the end?)

Hebrews 6:4-6: "It is impossible for those who were *enlightened, have tasted the heavenly gift, have become partakers of the Holy Spirit, have tasted the good Word of God, and the powers of the age to come, IF they FALL AWAY,* to renew them to repentance; since they crucify *AGAIN* for themselves the Son of God, and put Him to an open shame." (Speaking of believers who fall away!)

Hebrews 10:38-39: *"The just will live by faith. If any believer DRAWS BACK, My soul has no pleasure in him. But, we are not of those who draw back to PERDITION; but of those who believe to the SAVING of the soul."*

Chapter II

Distortion of *all, world* and *elect*

The words ALL and WORLD occur many times in the New Testament Scriptures—WORLD multiple times and ALL a lot more. John Calvin could somehow detect that the two words had DIFFERENT connotations in different passages. (???) In those passages that were vital to his theological position, those words became limited to the Elect. In all other cases, all meant all and world meant world. *WHO granted John Calvin the authority to make such rules? Manipulation of Scripture is a SURE SIGN of dishonesty! WHY* would God have the Bible authors to write *ALL* and/or *WORLD* if He actually meant Elect? If *ALL MEANS ALL* in one verse, why would it *NOT MEAN ALL* in other verses? And, if *WORLD MEANS WORLD in one passage, WHY WOULD IT NOT MEAN WORLD in all others? In revealing something regarding the Elect, why would God not have Bible writers to use the word Elect in every case? The term elect appears a DOZEN or more times in the New Testament books.* In *EVERY* case elect is clearly meant. So, why would God cloud the issue by having the authors use *all* or *world* in *SOME* passages, and *elect* in others—*if He actually meant elect in ALL of them? John Calvin deliberately distorted the Scriptures, in order to maintain HIS devilish doctrines, and horrific heresies.* If those New Testament book authors did not write what God *INSTRUCTED* them to write, *they either disobeyed the Holy Spirit, or, the Holy Spirit led them in the wrong direction! The Holy Spirit NEVER MISLED any Bible writer, but instead INSPIRED them to record Bible Truth. Calvin and Palmer MANIPULATED the Scriptures.* They literally *REWROTE* portions of God's Word.

9

Actually, *they MANIPULATED the religious MINDS of multitudes of gullible people to accept THEIR theology. I rightly use the term gullible, because, if people seriously scrutinize Calvin's doctrines in LIGHT of Holy Scripture, and do so with an honest mind, they cannot continue to believe such theological garbage.* To hold onto Calvinist doctrine, people have to deny some Scripture passages and distort many others—*just like Calvin and Palmer.*

Let us look at some of the *all* and *world* Scriptures: Isaiah 53:6 says: *"ALL we, like sheep have gone astray; we have turned every one of us unto his own way; and THE LORD has laid on Him THE INIQUITY OF US ALL." Calvin contended that although ALL have gone astray, God did NOT lay the iniquity of us ALL on Christ—ONLY the iniquity of His Elect.* Thus, we are supposed to take Calvin's word for it that Isaiah *FAILED* to communicate God's *TRUE MESSAGE;* and trust Calvin to fill us in on what God *REALLY* meant. (?????) *Calvin the LIAR!*

John 1:29: "John, [the Baptizer,] saw Christ coming to him, and said [to some of his disciples], 'Behold, the Lamb of God, *Who takes away the sins of the WORLD.'" Edwin Palmer ARGUED that the word world there could NOT have meant EVERY human being populating earth;* because we know that *Jesus died ONLY for God's Elect.* How would Edwin Palmer *KNOW* such a thing? *Neither Calvin nor Palmer ever produced one Scripture passage proving that Christ shed His blood ONLY for a few.* But, *both did a lot of arguing that their theology was correct; and did a whole lot of lying about it too!*

John 3:16-17 states that: "God so loved the *WORLD* that He gave His only-begotten-Son, so that whosoever believes on Him should *NOT PERISH*, but [should] have everlasting life...God sent His Son into the *WORLD*, not

10

to condemn the *WORLD*; but that the *WORLD* through Him might be *SAVED.*" Having arrived upon earth, did Christ enter *INTO THE ELECT*, or into human society? When does world *JUST* mean world? In John 3:16-17, the word *WORLD* has the very same meaning in *EACH* instance. So how could John Calvin and Edwin Palmer claim that the *WORLD* which God loved was *ONLY THE ELECT?* That Scripture could read: "God so loved every human being in the sinful world system, that He gave His only-begotten-Son, so that whosoever in the sinful world system believes upon Him would not perish, but would have everlasting life. For, God sent His Son into the fallen world system, not to condemn people in that system, but that all in that system through Him might be saved." *Everybody—not just certain Elect ones!*

In John Calvin's mind, *WORLD* does not mean the same in each biblical case. In one place it might mean God's Elect; in another the sinful social system; and in still another the earth itself. The Greek word rendered world in that John passage is kosmos—social system— which means all human beings inhabiting this planet. The original Greek means orderly arrangement, *and is sometimes actually applied to the universe.* The context will determine which of the two uses—people or planet. However, *KOSMOS NEVER REFERS TO* a small portion of this planet's population! *Calvin and Palmer LIED!*

The Calvinists also *PLAY* on the word *MANY*—trying to prove that Christ died *ONLY* for *SOME*—not all. They use Romans 5:15: "If by the offense of one man *MANY* be dead in sin, much more, the grace of God and God's gift of grace by one Man, Jesus Christ, *ABOUNDED TO MANY.*" Calvinists claim that *MANY refers to a limited number of people, and cannot mean every human being* on earth. However, Paul used the same *WORD MANY* in *referring to people God offers grace to just as he did the number of people who are lost in Adam!* That means if the *MANY* God offers His grace to are the *ELECT ONLY, then the MANY who fell in Adam would also be limited to the SAME small number of people. But, Paul used the word MANY of both the lost and those who are offered salvation. ALL are lost, so ALL can be saved!*

The same principle can be seen in Romans 5:18-19. "By the offense [the sin] of *ONE* man [Adam], judgment came upon *ALL* men to condemnation; even so, by the righteousness of *ONE,* [Jesus Christ] the free gift came upon *ALL* men unto justification of life. For, just as by one man's [Adam's] disobedience the *MANY* were made sinners, so by the obedience of One [Christ] will *MANY* be made righteous." Paul used those words *MANY* and *ALL* interchangeably—*proving that the same MANY and ALL who were condemned by Adam's one transgression were offered salvation through Jesus Christ's sacrifice.* Calvin's arguments, then, are just a bunch of religious mumbo-jumbo—instigated by the devil himself.

In 2 Corinthians 5:14, Paul wrote: "We thus judge that if One [Christ] died for *ALL,* then *ALL* were dead." The literal Greek: "...if the one [Christ] on behalf of *ALL* died, *THEN ALL DIED.*" When Christ died on our behalf, God saw us dying *IN UNION WITH* Him: When He died, we died. *Palmer said if Jesus died for ALL, every person would automatically be saved. Palmer defeated his own purpose by that argument; for even the Elect remain lost until they accept what Jesus did for them! Paul did not say the lost actually received their salvation at the time Jesus died*—but that His death *PROVIDED SALVATION FOR ALL the lost.* Salvation is available to every human being on earth. *But, only people who believe the Gospel message will actually be* saved. It is not automatic.

12

First Timothy 4:10 proves that Bible Truth: "*GOD IS SAVIOR OF ALL MEN*—especially of those who believe." That word *ESPECIALLY* means *IN PARTICULAR*, and to *THE GREATEST DEGREE*. Salvation is available to *ALL*, but *BELIEVERS IN PARTICULAR* will obtain salvation *to the GREATEST DEGREE*. All of Calvinism is a big lie!

Romans 6:6 says that *we were crucified with Christ. But His crucifixion occurred nearly two thousand years ago—long before we even existed. Being crucified WITH Christ simply means our being IDENTIFIED with Him in His crucifixion, death, burial and resurrection. And that is offered to ALL—not just to Calvin's SELECT ELECT!*

I noticed that in *ALL* of Edwin Palmer's arguments, in his explaining how certain passages refer only to the Elect—and not to *ALL*—he would always use passages other than the one he was discussing to prove his point. He could not glean from the words of the verses under discussion that God's Elect *ONLY* was meant. He could not *SQUEEZE* Limited Atonement out of those universal Scripture passages that used *ALL* or *WORLD*—although he claimed those passages simply could not mean what they literally stated. He tried to inject that concept into certain Scriptures by appealing to other Scriptures he claimed did teach that the Lord died only for the Elect: But, provided no real proof from those passages either!

First Timothy 2:1 *DEMANDS* of believers: "That first of all, supplications, prayers, intercessions, and, giving of thanks be made for *ALL MEN*." And, 1 Timothy 2:3-4 explains God's reason: "This is good and acceptable in the sight of God our Savior—Who will have *ALL* men to be *SAVED*, and to come to the knowledge of the truth." Paul taught in 1 Timothy 2:5-6: "There is one God, and one Mediator between God and men—*Which is the Man*

13

Christ Jesus; Who gave Himself a ransom for ALL men." ALL of these passages use the word *ALL—NOT ELECT.* Thus, it is evident that both Paul and God *MEANT ALL* human beings—*NOT* just an arbitrarily selected few!

Paul said God wants *ALL* men to be *SAVED.* And, to provide salvation for *ALL,* Jesus Christ gave Himself a *RANSOM FOR ALL.* Had Paul meant the Elect only, he would have said the Elect only. But being *INSPIRED* by the Holy Spirit, Paul knew which word was appropriate to get the Gospel message across. John Calvin the liar!

There is not a hint anywhere in Scripture that God wants only a few to be saved—and all others to be lost! Second Peter 3:9: *"The Lord is not slack concerning His promise, as some count slackness; but is long-suffering toward us, not willing that any should perish, but that ALL should come to repentance."*
Both Calvin and Palmer said Peter referred *ONLY* to the Elect in that passage—for God *DOES* want some to perish in Hell forever for His glory. And God chose that eternal fate for them at His discretion—not theirs. (???)

In 1 John 2:2, John said: "Christ is the propitiation for our sins: And, not for our sins only, but also for the *SINS OF THE WHOLE WORLD." Both Calvin and Palmer insisted that, WHOLE WORLD THERE, referred to other Elect believers scattered over the planet. John could not have meant EVERY lost person on earth. But, the word WORLD in 1 John 5:19 did mean the lost—Calvin said.*

Both Calvin and Palmer were MADMEN—possessed by a spirit not from above. For, the Holy Spirit would not have INSPIRED those demonic doctrines! Only the devil would push theology that arbitrarily puts people in Hell. Calvinism is demonic—*That entire theological system!*

14

Chapter III

Calvin's lying and accusing I

John Calvin *DECEIVED HIMSELF* with his demonic falsehoods. Then, he cursed *LARGE PORTIONS OF THE CHURCH with those falsehoods for five hundred years. The truth of that comment becomes apparent by looking at JOHN CALVIN'S COMMENTS upon* Exodus 32:32-33. His doctrinal position has been detrimental to not only the church, but to *GOD'S REPUTATION* as well!

Calvin's discussion of that passage reveals both his theological stance, and its reflection on God's character, PLUS its deceptive power within so much of the church. (All derived from John Calvin's Bible Commentaries.)

The primary purpose of John Calvin in dealing with that passage was to *PROVE* that the names of the Elect *CANNOT* be blotted out of the Book of Life. Calvin piled lie upon lie in that pathetic display of his stupidity!

Notice the EXTENT to which that man was willing to go, in order to maintain his claim: "What follows may in many respects appear to be *absurd* [Calvin referring to what Moses had said *under Holy Spirit inspiration!*]; for Moses both imperiously lays down the law to God, and in his eager impetuosity, *SEEKS* to overthrow, as far as he can, God's *eternal counsel*, and inconsiderately *robs God of His justice*. Surely, all must condemn the *PRIDE* of Moses' address—'*UNLESS You spare those offenders, count me* [Moses] *not as one of Your servants.*' Nor can there seem to be less of *FOLLY* in that attempt to bring to nothing God's eternal *PREDESTINATION*. Nor would I, indeed, deny, *THAT MOSES WAS CARRIED AWAY* by such vehemence that *he speaks like one possessed* [*BY*

15

A DEMON?]. Assuredly, there was nothing less present to the mind of Moses than to dictate to the Lord; nor, if he had been asked, would he have said that what God had decreed, respecting His Elect, before the creation of the world, could be overthrown... Moses, arrogating far too much to himself, he throws himself forward as [his] people's surety, and *FORGETS* that he is predestined to salvation by God's immutable counsel... Nor was Moses the only one who has been thus carried away; but Paul has gone even further [than Moses], expressing himself thus in writing, after full premeditation, 'I could [?] wish that I [Paul] myself were accursed from Christ *FOR* my [Jewish] brethren (Romans 9:3).'" (Then it gets worse.)

"*God so far accommodates Himself to our ignorance!* Let therefore the solution that I [Calvin] have advanced hold good—*that their petition was SO CONFUSED, that in the vehemence of their ardor THEY DID NOT SEE* the contradiction; *just like men beside themselves* [crazy]... By that Book, in which *GOD IS SAID* to have [recorded] His Elect, it *MUST BE* understood, metaphorically, His decree. But, that expression which Moses uses, asking to be blotted out of the number of the pious [the Elect], is an *INCORRECT ONE; since it cannot be that one who has been once elected should ever be reprobated...* [???] David uses two expressions with that very same sense: 'Blotted out, and not written': '*LET THEM BE BLOTTED OUT* of the Book of Life, and *NOT BE WRITTEN* with the RIGHTEOUS (Psalms 69:28).' Now, we cannot infer any changes in the counsel of God [eternal predestination]; but this phrase is merely equivalent to saying that God will at length make it manifest that the reprobate, who for [merely] a season *are counted among the number of the Elect*, [but,] in no respect belong to the body of the church... Thus the secret catalogue [book] in which the *ELECT* have been written, is contrasted by Ezekiel 13:9

16

with that external profession, which is often deceitful. Justly, therefore, did Christ bid His disciples to rejoice, because their names are written in heaven [according to Luke 10:20]; for, albeit the counsel of God, whereby we are predestined to salvation, is incomprehensible to us. Nevertheless, (as Paul wrote,) this seal stands sure: 'The Lord knows those who are His (2 Timothy 2:19).'"

NONE of those passages say Christians CANNOT BE LOST AGAIN—AND BECOME UNSAVED! Exodus 32:33: "Whoever has sinned against Me [God], him *WILL* I blot out [of The Book of Life]." Calvin said: "In these words, God *ADAPTS HIMSELF* to the *COMPREHENSION* of the human mind by His saying: 'Him [the person who sins] will I blot out': For, hypocrites [Where did God mention hypocrites?] make such a false profession of His name, that *they are not counted as aliens* [as reprobates] *until God openly renounces them*: And, hence, their manifest rejection [by God] is called erasure [blotting out]... God *REPROVES* the preposterous request of Moses." (????)

God did *NOT* rebuke Moses, but identified those He would *BLOT OUT* of that Book of Life—all rebels! *Calvin tried to DISARM the message of those verses by saying that Moses' words were ABSURD.* However, rather than reproving Moses, the *LORD* assured him: "Whoever has sinned against Me, him will I blot out of My book."

Contrast GOD'S comment with Calvin's comments on Moses' REQUEST and God's RESPONSE to Moses. John Calvin *ACCUSED* Moses of laying down the law to God; of trying to overthrow God's eternal counsel (meaning His *UNALTERABLE PREDESTINATION OF THE ELECT*); and inconsiderately robbing God of justice. Calvin also insinuated that Moses was guilty of *PRIDE* and *FOLLY*. He even suggested that Moses' words indicated that he was *POSSESSED*. (By what?) *Moses was either ignorant of the Bible Truth that God had determined even before creation that certain people would be saved and others remain lost by God's arbitrary decision; or forgot that he himself was one of God's CHOSEN—whose name could NOT be blotted out of God's Book.* Then, Calvin injected one of his favorite *unscriptural words* into the doctrinal mix. It was inexcusable that John Calvin spoke *EVIL* of Moses, but he certainly crossed the line of honesty *BY ACCUSING GOD OF LYING—contending that the Divine response to Moses in* Exodus 32:33 *was an adaptation to, or accommodation of, Moses' ignorance.* That means God stooped down to *MOSES' LEVEL* of understanding. God used the same words Moses used because neither Moses nor we could understand His incomprehensible, *SECRET counsel* regarding the *ELECT. By claiming that God ADAPTED HIS WORDS to Moses' ignorance, Calvin accused God of committing the very same errors he said Moses had committed.* Thus, calling God a liar!

Why would Jehovah lower Himself to Moses' level of understanding? *Would that OCCASION not have been a good time to correct Moses' theology* (if Moses had been wrong)? Instead of enlightening Moses that the names of the Elect could not be blotted out of the Book of Life, "The *LORD* said to Moses: 'Whoever has sinned against Me, *I WILL BLOT OUT OF MY BOOK*.'" Whereas, Calvin contended that names could not be blotted out of that Book, *God confirmed that He Himself would blot out the names of those who transgressed against Him!* Will you believe, and agree with, John Calvin, or Almighty God? Remember that Calvin accused Moses of being *absurd*, of *having pride, acting in folly*, and *being possessed. He also said that Moses was CONFUSED and INCORRECT in his REQUEST to God.* That was *PREPOSTEROUS* and *INCONSIDERATE* of Moses. Then, *Calvin EVEN accused the Almighty of the SAME mistakes he said Moses had made.* God accommodating Himself to Moses' *LEVEL* of understanding essentially means that God agreed with Moses in his errors—The logical conclusion of Calvin's claim. *IF* Moses' words there were indeed *INCORRECT, THEN MOSES LIED.* And that would have to mean that *either Moses disobeyed the Holy Spirit's inspiration, or, the Holy Spirit gave Moses the wrong words. IF* Moses did lie, and God adapted Himself to Moses' words, then God lied too! Thus, John *Calvin essentially ACCUSED God Himself of lying!* Before discounting my comments, consider again what God Himself had Moses to pen in Exodus 32:33: "Whosoever has sinned against Me, him will I blot out of My Book." Moses right! Calvin wrong!

Calvin *ADAMANTLY* contended that no name of any Elect could be removed from the Book of Life, whereas God said that He both could and *would BLOT OUT* the name of *ANY* Elect one who deliberately sinned against Him. *Multitudes being fooled by Calvin's theology does not make Clavin's theology correct!* What say you?

John Calvin's comments on Exodus 32:32-33 erode people's faith in God's Word. Think now: Calvin's claim that names *CANNOT* be blotted out of the Book of Life, even though *GOD* Himself said that *HE* would blot out the names of people who sinned against Him, makes it clear that John Calvin meant that one portion of God's Word is not true. At least that one Scripture passage is *NOT* Holy-Spirit-inspired. And that would suggest that *Moses, God's Word, and the Holy Spirit all LIED. Those whom we have been taught to put our trust in LIED!* John Calvin's words trumped the words of Moses; and *EVEN THE WORDS OF MEMBERS OF THE GODHEAD!* So, how can we Christians trust any of the rest of what the Bible says? (If Calvin's theology were correct!)

John Calvin's theology has been believed and even *LAUDED* by multitudes of *PEOPLE* and *CHURCHES* for *FIVE CENTURIES. NOW,* it is my calling, and God-given privilege, to *DEBUNK* this and numerous other Calvinist falsehoods—shameful demonic Calvinist falsehoods!

In my *RESEARCH* of John Calvin's "Institutes of the Christian Religion" and his Bible Commentaries, I have observed at least three *TERMS* Calvin resorted to when he ran into a biblical *TRUTH* that threatened to *EXPOSE* his *DEMONIC* errors. First, and foremost, was the term *SECRET WILL,* or *SECRET COUNSEL.* Calvin repeatedly attempted to counter all objections to his false doctrines by appealing to what he called *THE SECRET COUNSEL OF GOD.* Upon finding no actual biblical support for his claims (which problem John Calvin frequently faced), he would always fall back on that crutch of God's *SECRET WILL.* Deuteronomy 29:29 says secret things belong to God—indicating that we can know *ONLY* the things God chooses to reveal! So, how did Calvin *DISCOVER* God's *SECRET WILL?* Moreover, why did God's *SECRET WILL ALWAYS BACK JOHN CALVIN'S THEOLOGY? WHAT A CONVENIENT THEOLOGICAL COINCIDENCE!!!!!!!!!!*

ACCOMMODATION or *ADAPTATION* was yet another word Calvin used in defense of his *FALSE DOCTRINES.* But, his contention that God adapted His Words to the limited understanding of the human race—*God getting down on our level of comprehension*—implies that some of God's Words recorded in the Bible *DO NOT EXPRESS HIS TRUE WILL.* To understand what God really meant to communicate to humanity, *we must rely on Calvin's interpretations—not what the Bible actually says.* (????) If words mean anything, it is obvious that John Calvin was the liar—the devil's *PRIZED,* deceived, mouthpiece! *HOLY SCRIPTURE IS GOD'S INSPIRED REVELATION OF*

TRUTH; NOT A MEANS OF HIDING THAT TRUTH! GOD HAS TO OPEN OUR EYES TO BIBLE TRUTH! No human being can just *DISCOVER* Bible Truth. And, if anybody knows how to say what He *REALLY* means to say, *THE ALL-WISE* God does. Calvin was the *DUMMY!* Nor can I conceive of our Creator playing *TRICKS* on His creation. The devil is the trickster—through demonic Calvinism!

A third term Calvin added to that theological mix to confuse Bible readers about Bible Truth was the word *HYPOCRITE.* Supposedly, those whose names God said He would blot out of the Book of Life were not the Elect anyway. They were just *HYPOCRITES.* Strangely, *in the passages that mention certain names being blotted out of the Book of Life, the word hypocrite NEVER appears.* The term is only mentioned in Calvin's explanations of those texts! Moreover, *I have to ask how a name can be erased from a list it was never registered on in the first place. If none of those hypocrites were God's Elect, then they were never written in the Book of Life! Their names could not have been removed from a BLANK PAGE.*

Calvin challenged the CORE TRUTHS of Scripture in the development and maintenance of his theology. What follows is proof of that truth. Tucked neatly in Calvin's *COMMENTARY* on Exodus 32:32-33 is his distortion of Psalms 69:28 and Ezekiel 13:9. King David mentioned blotting names from that Book of Life, and John Calvin accused David of the *SAME* ignorance that Moses had *SUPPOSEDLY EXHIBITED.* Psalms 69:21 *is a prophecy of our Savior's CRUCIFIXION. On the cross Jesus Christ experienced the fulfillment of David's detailed prophecy:* "They gave Me gall for My meat; and in My thirst, they gave Me vinegar to drink (Matthew 27:34; John 19:28-30)." That prophecy continued: "*Let* [Christ's accusers] *BE BLOTTED OUT of the book of the living, and NOT BE*

WRITTEN WITH THE RIGHTEOUS (Psalms 69:28)." *But, Calvin contended that no name can be blotted out of the Book of Life, no matter what the Holy Scriptures tell us.* That *REVEALS* Calvin's *OUTRIGHT DISHONESTY!*

John Calvin also referred to the prophecy in Psalms 109:8; which obviously refers to Judas—who betrayed Jesus: "Let his days be few; and, let *ANOTHER* take his office." Before the Day of Pentecost, Peter remembered that prophecy. Acts 1:15-26 says: "In those days, Peter stood up, in the midst of the disciples, then said—(*the number of names being about a hundred-twenty*)—'Men and brethren, this Scripture had to be fulfilled—which *THE HOLY GHOST SPOKE BY THE MOUTH OF DAVID* [David wrote what he wrote *UNDER INSPIRATION* of the Holy Spirit—so how could David have been confused?], concerning Judas, who was guide unto those who took Jesus. *Because Judas was numbered with us, and had obtained part of this* [Gospel] ministry. He purchased a field with the reward of iniquity [thirty pieces of silver]; then, falling headlong, he burst asunder, in the midst, and all of his bowels gushed out. And, it was known to all of those dwellers at Jerusalem; because that field is called in their proper tongue "Aceldama"; [or] "The field of blood." Because, it is written in the Book of Psalms: "Let his [Judas'] habitation be desolate, and let no one dwell therein: And his office [of apostleship] let another take." Wherefore of these men, who have accompanied us all that time our Lord Jesus Christ went in and out among us, beginning from the baptism of John, to that same day, when He was taken up from us [speaking of His ascension], *MUST ONE* be ordained to be a witness with us of His resurrection.' And so they appointed two men—Joseph, called Barsabbas, surnamed Justus, and Matthias. Then they prayed, and said: 'You, [Oh] Lord, Who knows the hearts of all men, let us know which of these men You have chosen—that he may take part of this ministry and apostleship; *from which Judas by his transgression fell, that he might go to his OWN PLACE.'* [Transgression strips one of *MORE* than a mere office.] And they cast their lots; and the lot fell upon Matthias; and he was numbered with the other eleven apostles."

Yet speaking of Judas, Psalms 109:13 *reported this*: "Let his *POSTERITY* [his children] be cut off; and in the generation following, let their name be *BLOTTED OUT*." *If even Judas' offspring were to BE BLOTTED OUT, then the same would certainly APPLY TO JUDAS!* Moreover, *the BLOTTING OUT could not have referred ONLY to the MEMORY of Judas—because both his name and tragic history are recorded in the Book of Acts.* And, if Judas' name was to be *BLOTTED OUT* of the Book of Life, *then his name must have been written in it!* So, names in the Book of Life can indeed be blotted out of it!

In Ezekiel 13:9, *GOD* said plainly: "My hand will be upon the prophets who see vanity, and who divine lies: They will *NOT* be in the assembly of My people; neither will they *BE WRITTEN IN THAT REGISTER* of the house of Israel; neither will they enter into the land of Israel." *Names can be either SUBTRACTED FROM or ADDED TO the Book of Life! Holy Scripture proves the reality of that fact—though Calvin ADAMANTLY contended otherwise.* John Calvin was a pathetic lying hypocrite!

Calvin rebutted those objections by saying: "*Without doubt we must understand the CONTRAST between the true members of the Church and hypocrites* [No mention of *HYPOCRITES* in Ezekiel 13:9, or any other Scripture passage addressing that *BLOTTING-OUT* subject!], *who* [only] *PRETEND to the name of God; because, as God's election is ETERNAL, his sons were written in the book*

23

of life before the creation of the world. [What Scripture passage says that?] But, [Ezekiel] says they will not *BE WRITTEN*, which seems *absurd* [the same word used to discredit Moses' prayer in Exodus 32:32]. But, Ezekiel here *ACCOMMODATES* [There is John Calvin's favorite word once again!] his language to the usual custom of mankind. The language of the Psalms is even harsher: 'Let them *BE BLOTTED OUT of* the Book of Life, *SINCE* [??] they are not written among the just [the righteous] (Psalms 69:28).'" John Calvin wrote: "*since they are not written,*" But the Bible says: "*Let them not be written.*"

"*It cannot happen that he who is once written in the Book of Life can EVER be blotted out* [Where does God's Word tell *ANY* such lie?]. Ezekiel also wrote: 'They *will NOT BE WRITTEN in the writings of the house of Israel'*: Because, *FOR A TIME* they *SEEMED TO BE* among the number of the pious [the righteous]: Hence a change of expression is here used, but only in *ACCOMMODATION* to the rudeness of our human minds." But, *Ezekiel did not say that names can neither be added to the Book of Life nor deleted from it.* That was Calvin's speculation.

"Jesus said that none [of the twelve apostles] is lost except the son of Perdition [Judas] (John 17:12). That expression is not strictly proper; but, it is by no means obscure: Because Judas was not numbered among the *SHEEP* of Christ because he *WAS ONE TRULY* [Calvin's personal speculation—*There is no Bible PROOF of that.*] but [*ONLY*] because *HE HELD A PLACE AMONG THEM.* [What did Calvin mean by that?] In one more passage, where the Lord says that [Judas] *WAS ELECTED WITH THE APOSTLES, THAT REFERENCE IS MADE ONLY TO THE OFFICE* [*OF APOSTLE—NOT TO HIS ELECTION TO SALVATION. Once again, THAT IS MERE SPECULATION on John Calvin's part. No Scripture teaches that.*]: 'Have

24

not I chosen you twelve,' says He, 'and one of you *IS* a devil (John 6:70).' [*IS A DEVIL—NOT ALWAYS WAS A DEVIL!* John 17:12—*No disciple HAD PERISHED except JUDAS—JUDAS HAD NOT ALWAYS BEEN PERISHED!*] *Jesus chose Judas to the office of apostle. But, when he spoke of election to salvation, Jesus altogether excluded him from the number of the Elect: 'I speak not of you all, for, I KNOW whom I have chosen (John 13:18).'* [*Judas fell AFTER being chosen!*] If anyone confounds the term *ELECTION* in those two passages [Where does the Bible speak of different kinds of election?], *he will miserably entangle himself* [*in DOCTRINAL ERROR*]; whereas if he distinguishes between [two different kinds of election], then nothing can be plainer to him [than John Calvin's supposed doctrinal truth—which in reality is a big lie]. I deny not however, that the *HOLY SPIRIT SOMETIMES ACCOMMODATES HIS LANGUAGE* to our feeble human capacity [to understand Bible Truth]; as when He says, 'They will not be in the assembly of My people; nor will they *BE WRITTEN IN* the register of the house of Israel (Ezekiel 13:9)'; *AS IF* [implying that Ezekiel's words in that passage were incorrect] God were now *BEGINNING TO WRITE* the names of those whom He counts among His people in the Book of Life; whereas we know on the testimony of Christ, that *names of the children of God were written in the Book of Life FROM THE BEGINNING* (Luke 10:20). [*WHERE IS* "from the beginning" in Luke 10:20?] Ezekiel's words simply indicate abandonment of those who *SEEMED* to have a chief place among the Elect." (*John Calvin only SEEMED to have the truth!*)

"We know that *those who are adopted to the hope of salvation were written* [in the Book of Life] *BEFORE the foundation of the world* (Ephesians 1:4). [Ephesians 1:4 says nothing about names being written in the Book of Life. *That was the invention of Calvin and Satan.*] God's eternal purpose of election is *INCOMPREHENSIBLE* [to men; *yet, Calvin said he knew all about it!*]. *So it is said in ACCOMMODATION TO THE IMPERFECTION OF OUR HUMAN UNDERSTANDING that those whom God enrolls among his people are written in the Book of Life.* On the other hand, people whom God *REJECTS*, and casts out of His church, are said to be *blotted out.*" [Again, I ask: "*How can one's name be blotted out of a book that HIS OR HER NAME WAS NOT RECORDED IN?*" John Calvin called Ezekiel and the Holy Spirit liars. *Calvin was the liar, and multitudes of people have been hoodwinked by his lies for centuries.* Time to eliminate Calvinism!]

Refer to Calvin's "*Institutes of the Christian Religion*" book 3, chapter 24, section 9. Calvin cleverly muddied the *CLEAR* waters of Psalms 69:28 and Ezekiel 13:9 by implying that being blotted out is *A MERE FIGURE OF SPEECH*, whereas being written in the Book of Life was actual. Psalms 69:28 and Ezekiel 13:9 are *NOT* figures of speech, but are *God's clear revelation of Bible Truth.* Thus, *the possibility of names of the Elect being blotted out of the Book of Life is just as real as names having been written in it!* Neither did David, nor Ezekiel, imply that names of the Elect were written before creation. In fact, both Scriptures indicate that names can be added to or subtracted from the Book of Life at any time.

Also notice that *IT TOOK PAGES* of commentary for Calvin to explain a few verses of Scripture. That within itself is a *SURE* indication of the struggle Calvin had in defending his theology. Had he only been *HONEST*, his written works would have been *much less voluminous,* and *much more reliable!* John Calvin just made all that stuff up. *There is not a shred of scriptural evidence that any of his theology is correct.* Rather, *it is a demonic lie!*

Chapter IV

Calvin's lying and accusing II

I will begin by focusing on one word Calvin used in his comments on Exodus 32:32-33. In that quote a few pages back Calvin claimed the Holy Spirit *SOMETIMES* uses language in Scripture that is *ACCOMMODATED* to the *FEEBLE* capacity of the human race to understand Bible Truth. Calvin claimed the Holy Spirit *SOMETIMES USES VEILED* language. But *WHY* would the Holy Spirit *ONLY SOMETIMES* accommodate our *FEEBLE* capacity? Why not at *ALL* times? *IF IT IS OUR FEEBLE CAPACITY WHICH MAKES IT NECESSARY FOR THE HOLY SPIRIT TO SPEAK IN VEILED LANGUAGE IN CERTAIN BIBLE CASES, WHY NOT IN ALL BIBLE CASES?* Why is it that *OUR LOW CAPACITY TO UNDERSTAND* is problematic *ONLY* regarding certain Scripture passages? Is that not proof that Calvin was just pushing another demonic lie? Why do people *BLINDLY CLING* to Calvin's falsehoods?

John Calvin's *SOMETIMES* theology *is nothing but a religious farce—because those SOMETIMES-THE-HOLY-SPIRIT-ACCOMMODATES-OUR-FEEBLE-CAPACITY-TO-UNDERSTAND-SCRIPTURE-CASES have only to do with those passages that concern John Calvin's questionable doctrines! It was not necessary for NON-THREATENING passages.* Our supposed mental *FEEBLENESS* was not a problem in those cases! *If my bringing to the reader's attention John Calvin's DISHONEST DEALINGS fails to activate their WARNING signal, or turn on their HERESY caution light, the reader's spiritual battery level must be very LOW or altogether DEPLETED. It CANNOT BE mere coincidence that IT IS ONLY IN those Scripture passages that hold information that POSES A THREAT to Calvin's theology that the Holy Spirit USES VEILED LANGUAGE to accommodate our LOW capacity to understand Bible Truth. If we BELIEVERS TRULY ARE THAT INEPT, then how can we know WHICH Scripture passages are okay AS WRITTEN, AND WHICH ONES require John Calvin's INTERPRETATION to make them understandable to us? That would make our Bible study a frustrating activity: EVERY Christian home would need Calvin's 22 volume Bible Commentary set, along with his "Institutes of the Christian Religion"* monstrosity—one thousand pages!

Calvin's ACCOMMODATION THEOLOGY implies that the literal wording of some Scriptures communicates the opposite of God's actual will regarding the matters dealt with in those Scriptures. Even though God said plainly that He would *BLOT OUT* of the Book of Life the names of transgressors, in reality no name can ever be blotted out of the Book of Life (according to John Calvin). The logical conclusion of such theology would obviously be: *Sometimes the Bible as written actually lies!* Of course, not all Scripture passages need John Calvin's *SPECIAL INTERPRETATION.* Calvin could somehow detect which Bible passages needed his Scripture-tweaking abilities, and which ones did not. Strangely, only the Scriptures that challenge his theology needed his unique talent of totally reversing the literal wording of those Scriptures. Calvin never found one Scripture passage that actually says names *CANNOT* be blotted out of the Book of Life. Instead, he was challenged by several passages plainly teaching that names both can and will be deleted from the Book of Life! However, Calvin argued that he knew God's *SECRET WILL,* which happens *TO BE OPPOSITE OF WHAT IS LITERALLY WRITTEN* in certain Scripture passages. Calvin's interpretations would be needed for *A PROPER UNDERSTANDING OF THE LITERAL WORDS*

WRITTEN IN THOSE BIBLE PASSAGES (In the Inspired Scriptures!). *And millions of people have fallen for that Calvinist GARBAGE over the past five hundred years!*

Romans 11:5 says in the literal Greek that in Paul's day *some NEWLY ELECT had come into being by grace.* *"ELECT HAVING JUST COME INTO BEING MUST MEAN THAT NEW NAMES HAD BEEN ADDED TO THE BOOK OF LIFE!* Therefore, Calvin accusing Moses, David, and Ezekiel of being *CONFUSED* about that *BLOTTING-OUT* issue, proves that Calvin himself was either *IGNORANT* of Bible Truth, or was an outright *HYPOCRITE!*

John Calvin said King David was *CONFUSED* about what he wrote in Psalms 69:28, whereas in Acts 1:16, Peter said that David *PROPHESIED* in Psalms 109:6-13 *BY THE HOLY SPIRIT* about *JUDAS'* transgression, and fall. Therefore, what King David wrote in Psalms 69:28 about names being blotted out of the Book of Life must have been *INSPIRED BY THE HOLY SPIRIT too!*

John Calvin's rebuke of Ezekiel was also a slam on *HOLY SPIRIT INSPIRATION!* How dare that man accuse those men moved by the Holy Spirit of being confused? Ezekiel was no more *CONFUSED* than was King David! Calvin was the *DECEIVED, CONFUSED, HYPOCRITE!*

Most Christians are TOTALLY UNAWARE of just how HYPOCRITICAL John Calvin was. Moreover, despite his reputation as being a *theologian par excellence,* he was *NOT* really all that smart. Accusing the All-Wise God of *BEING UNABLE TO COMMUNICATE WHAT HE REALLY MEANT TO COMMUNICATE IN HIS WRITTEN WORD;* or *CALLING HIM WHO CANNOT LIE* (Titus 1:2, Hebrews 6:18, 1 John 2:21) a *LIAR* is *NOT* all that smart! Calvin was one of those that Romans 1:25 says turned God's Truth into a lie. *Calvinism is an INEXCUSABLE LIE!*

Let me show you a *PRIME* example of John Calvin›s *DISHONESTY* in dealing with the Scriptures. In book 1, chapter 17, sections 7, and 8, of his "Institutes of the Christian Religion," Calvin insisted that *"God overrules all creatures, even the devil himself—WHO DARED NOT attempt anything against Job without God's permission and command.* [*Permission yes; command no!*] Had Job turned [his attention] to those Chaldeans, by whom he [had been] plundered, [then Job] would instantly have been fired with revenge; but recognizing that it was the *WORK* of the *LORD,* Job solaced himself with this most *BEAUTIFUL SENTIMENT:* 'The Lord gave, and the Lord has *TAKEN* away; blessed be the name of the Lord (Job 1:21).'" *And that SENTIMENT is with us to this day!*

In that comment, you can see John Calvin's demonic sentiment by his considering it a beautiful thing that the LORD had taken away ALL of Job's children, goods and happiness—especially when the Bible says plainly that the devil was the one *AFFLICTING JOB!* But, to Calvin, what was recorded in God's Word made *NO* difference. *WHAT JOHN CALVIN WANTED TO BELIEVE WAS THE IMPORTANT THING.* John 10:10 says *THE DEVIL is the one who STEALS, KILLS,* and *DESTROYS—NOT GOD!*

Calvinism portrays God as a criminal. *And I am not trying to build a false case against John Calvin.* Book 1, chapter 18, sections 1 and 3, of Calvin's *INSTITUTES:* "From the first chapter of Job we *LEARN* that the devil appeared in God's presence *TO RECEIVE HIS ORDERS* [Where is that said?], *just as do those angels who obey God spontaneously. The manner and end[-results] were different, but still, the FACT IS that he* [the devil] *cannot attempt anything without the will of God.* But although afterwards his power to afflict that saint *SEEMS TO BE ONLY* bare permission [from God]; yet as the sentiment is true [?????], 'The Lord gave, and the Lord has taken away'; *as it has PLEASED the Lord, so it has been done*; [Those last eleven words were *ADDED* by John Calvin!] we infer that *GOD WAS THE AUTHOR OF THAT TRIAL*; of which the devil and wicked robbers were merely the instruments." *But, those trials being the devil's attempt to get Job to CURSE GOD*, James 1:13 comes into play: "Let *NO ONE* say when he is tempted, 'I am tempted by God': For, God cannot be tempted by evil: Nor does He Himself tempt anyone." So it is Calvin versus the Word of God once again. (Job 1:11, 4-5, 9—*the curse verses*.) *John Calvin was a hopeless, deceived, lying hypocrite!*

MORE LIES: "I would again remind *MY* readers that such a cavil [argument against *MY* doctrine] is directed not against me, but really against the Holy Spirit, Who certainly dictated this confession to that holy man Job: *'The Lord gave and the Lord HAS TAKEN AWAY'*; when, *after being plundered by robbers he acknowledges that their injustice and mischief was a just CHASTISEMENT from God*." In Job 1:8 and 2:3-4 *God BRAGGED on Job*. So why would God then chastise Job? *John Calvin was desperate to prove his point in that pathetic argument.*

By saying those things, it is clear that Calvin added to and took away from Holy Scripture at will; assuming liberties he allowed nobody else. *God's Word condemns those who TAMPER with His Word—so John Calvin was a CONDEMNED man!* Calvin still being popular among multitudes of church members today does not impress God—Whom Calvin lied on—and even accused of lying.

Neither Job nor any other Bible Book implies that the devil comes TO RECEIVE ORDERS FROM GOD. Rather, Scripture reveals that he shows up *UNINVITED. Neither does Job's Book imply that God gave the devil ORDERS*;

31

except LIMITATIONS ON WHAT HE COULD DO TO JOB! Moreover, *that account nowhere suggests that Satan's ATTACKS on Job were CHASTISEMENTS.* That Satanic concept came out of John Calvin's morbid mindset. He could somehow detect his theology written between the lines of Scripture, even when his theology diametrically opposed the words written on those Scripture lines.

Calvin's EXPLANATION of why he appealed to God's supposed SECRET WILL to come up with his SUPERIOR INTERPRETATIONS: "BECAUSE our [human] weakness cannot reach God's height, then any description which we receive of God MUST BE LOWERED to our capacity, IN ORDER TO BE INTELLIGIBLE [to us human beings]. And THE MODE OF LOWERING IS TO REPRESENT GOD NOT AS HE REALLY IS, BUT AS WE CONCEIVE HIM TO BE." (Institutes, book 1, chapter 17, section 13.)

But, *was Calvin NOT JUST AS HUMAN as the rest of us? Then, how did he soar beyond his human capacity to learn what the Holy Spirit had FAILED to reveal to us through Scripture?* What *POWER* did he use to tap into that realm beyond actual Bible revelation? Why would the Bible *HIDE* God's true character; and then *REVEAL* it to John Calvin by some secret means? *Implying that the true nature of God can be found only in Calvinism—the very opposite of clear Bible revelation! (HERESY!)*

I want to point out John Calvin's ultra-hypocrisy by *contrasting his AGREEING with Job's sentiment and his STERN REBUKE of Moses, David and Ezekiel, about the removal of names from God's Book of Life.* Throughout Moses' writings, you will not find *ONE* instance of God *REBUKING* Moses for statements about blotting names out of the Book of Life. Not one! The same can be said of what David and Ezekiel wrote, regarding the issue of name-blotting. Calvin chided Moses, David and Ezekiel over their *PLAIN* statements about blotting names out of the Book of Life; but he never even questioned Job's accusation of his own Creator of being the *SOLE* cause of Job's calamities. *Mind-boggling beyond belief!*

Why did John Calvin not CHIDE Job for making his comment, for which God did eventually rebuke Job? The Creator corrected Job's unethical view of Him, whereas Calvin accepted what God rebuked; then rebuked what God did not rebuke concerning the comments made by Moses, David and Ezekiel on name-blotting! *Does that not raise a QUESTION in your mind about John Calvin's honesty?* If not, why not? What was Calvin's reason for rejecting those comments God did not reject, and then *whole-heartedly backing Job's questionable comments, which God openly REBUKED? COMMENTS FOR WHICH JOB LATER REPENTED—CONFESSING THAT HE HAD SPOKEN OF THINGS HE KNEW NOTHING ABOUT!* That answer is simple—Moses, David and Ezekiel *ALL* made statements which contradicted John Calvin's doctrine, *whereas Job's comments agreed with Calvin's theology.*

Calvin deviously dismissed the Bible Truth found in the writings of Moses, David and Ezekiel—then brashly claimed the Holy Spirit Himself had dictated (inspired) Job's statement that God was the One Who plundered his possessions, killed his children and later destroyed his health. *Calvin had a demonically-twisted mind-set!*

After that exposure of Calvin's dishonesty, how can anybody ever again trust any part of Calvin's theology? Calvin was *WELL-EDUCATED* in the Hebrew and Greek languages, *so none of his underhanded manipulation of Scripture can be attributed to ignorance.* That man was deceitfully dishonest—making him an outright heretic! *How will the church respond to that indisputable truth?*

33

You do not have to take my bare word for all of this. Let us look at several revealing passages in the book of Job. *It will soon become CLEAR that those words which John Calvin contended were dictated by the Holy Spirit were the fruit of that pressure the devil had put on Job through all of his sufferings.* Of course, Job, not having access to the book written later about his experiences, he knew not that it was the devil, and not God, behind his afflictions. Calvin cleverly avoided passages in Job that reveal that Bible Truth. *IMAGINE THAT!*

Let us begin with Job 38:1-2: "The *LORD* answered Job out of a whirlwind, and said [In words that we can all understand even without John Calvin's help!]: *'Who is this who DARKENS counsel* [distorts God's Truth] *by his words without knowledge?'"* The *LORD* further said: "Will this one, who contends with the Almighty, correct Him? The one who rebukes God, let him answer it (Job 40:1-2)." Job 40:8: "Would you *ANNUL* My judgments? *Would you condemn Me* [God], *so that YOU* [Job] *might be justified?" That had to include Job claiming that God had "taken away."* Remember, Job had said: "If this is not God, *WHO* can it be (Job 9:24)?" Job was obviously devil-ignorant—just like many in the church today.

Besides Job's words in Job 1:21-22: "Naked I came out of my mother's womb and naked will I return. *THE LORD GAVE, AND THE LORD HAS TAKEN AWAY,"* Job *had UTTERED some other things about God which were untrue.* What words did God rebuke Job for? Dare look at Job 9:22-24, where Job said: "He [God] destroys the blameless, and the wicked." In addition: "If the scourge slays suddenly, God *LAUGHS* at the plight of innocent people. This earth is given into the hand of the wicked. He covers the faces of the judges. *If it is not GOD, WHO ELSE could it be?" Such is indisputable PROOF that Job thought God Himself was the Perpetrator of his terrible calamities.* However, Job 1:12-19 and 2:7 state plainly that the devil was both the designer and perpetrator of Job's woes. James 1:13 tells us God is *NOT* the author of our trials or temptations! So it was not God bringing all of those troubles on Job. The Book of Job itself says that it was the devil who brought all of those things on him. And the book also says: "In all of this, Job did not sin or charge God foolishly." But, although Job did not deliberately sin against God, he did make some unwise statements—*statements which God later REBUKED!*

Job 16:11 *shines even MORE LIGHT on Job's DARK words*: "God has delivered me to the ungodly [*and that without cause*], and turned me over to the hands of the wicked." Job obviously referred there to both his bodily sufferings, *AND* to his three so-called friends, *whom he CALLED miserable comforters* (Job 16:2), *forgers of lies, AND worthless physicians* (Job 13:4). *JOB TOUTED* his complete innocence before God, while accusing God of unjustly punishing him for reasons unknown—all the while maintaining his faith in God—as he expressed in Job 13:15: "Even though He slay me, yet will I trust in Him." Yet stating again: "Even so, I will defend my own [innocent] ways before Him." This and other comments by Job reveal that his *WORDS* were a *COMBINATION* of *TRUTH* and *ERROR*. The Lord rebuked Job's erroneous words, whereas John Calvin accepted them as *TRUTH*. Why? Because those words seemingly backed Calvin's demonic doctrines! What was Job's response to God's rebuke? Job 42:3: "You asked: 'Who is this who *HIDES* counsel without knowledge?' Therefore, *I have uttered what I did not understand; things too wonderful for me; which I did not know.*" Further stating in Job 42:5-6: "I have heard of You [God] by the hearing of the ear: But, now my eye sees You. Therefore, *I ABHOR MYSELF* and repent in dust and ashes." Repent of what? Saying all of those *ERRONEOUS* things about God! Why did John Calvin not consider all those passages when evaluating Job's statement in 1:21? God's rebuke surely included those *INFAMOUS* words—*"The LORD has taken away."* The book of Job states plainly that the devil was Job's attacker, not God! *Satan is the thief and murderer!*

Now I need to clear up another error. Some people point out God's statement that Job had spoken *RIGHT THINGS ABOUT HIM.* But when did God say that about Job? *AFTER JOB REPENTED! If Job had spoken all the right things about God BEFORE God rebuked him, then why the rebuke?* Obviously, God's rebuke straightened out Job's theology. *Only then did God say that Job had spoken right things about Him. Study ALL Scripture has to say about a subject before making any conclusions.*

Job 42:7-8: *"AFTER THE LORD HAD SPOKEN* those words [of rebuke] to Job, the *LORD* said to Eliphaz, the Temanite [Job's primary critic]: '*MY WRATH* is aroused against you and against your two friends; for you have not spoken of Me what is right like My servant Job has [spoken of Me *SINCE* I rebuked him]. Now, therefore, [I demand that you] take for yourselves seven bulls, and seven rams, and go to My servant Job, and offer up for yourselves a burnt offering: *THEN,* My servant Job will pray for you. For I will accept him—lest I deal with you according to your folly—because you have *NOT* spoken of Me what is *RIGHT, LIKE* My servant Job has [spoken about Me since I rebuked Him].'"

In Job 3:25, Job confessed that he had had a part in bringing all those calamities on himself through his fearful attitude: "For, *the thing that I greatly feared has come upon me; and what I was afraid of has come unto me."* Fear always opens the door to the devil's works of *stealing, killing,* and *destroying.* Fear also has torment (1 John 4:18). And Job was tormented for at least *TWO MONTHS*—Job 7:3: "I am made to possess *MONTHS OF VANITY* [unnecessary suffering]." Job also wished "that my words were written! Oh, that they were inscribed in a book (Job 19:23)!" Job's words were written; and we can read them today. God rebuked Job for some of his words—words Calvin taught were proof of his theology!

Moreover, Job's hardships were not a total loss. He did get double for his trouble—as one old saying goes. However, *I am sure Job did not want to go through any of that again.* Sometimes, *God does have to work IN US to correct our wrong thinking and talking, before He can deliver us OUT OF undesirable circumstances. That was certainly the case in Job's case.* However, *that does not mean that God brings those undesirable circumstances into our lives. But He does take advantage of the events in our lives, to help us learn how to live better lives.*

Job 42:10 says: "And the *LORD* turned the captivity of Job *WHEN* he prayed for his friends: Also, the *LORD GAVE* Job twice as much as he had before [his trials]." Job got healed, got a new ten-child family, and gained *DOUBLE* the possessions he previously possessed.

Job 42:11-13 *indicates that Job's family and friends had the same distorted view of God,* which Job had to repent of, but which Calvin accounted as sure proof of his doctrines: "They bemoaned him and comforted him over all the evil the *LORD* had brought upon him [???]: *Everyone also gave Job a piece of money, and everyone gave him an earring of gold.* So, the *LORD* blessed the latter end of Job more than his beginning: For, he had [*DOUBLE* the previous possessions]. He also had seven sons and three daughters." (*By that same woman?*)

"After this Job lived *ANOTHER* hundred-forty years, and saw his sons, and his sons' sons; *four generations.* And so, Job died, being old, and full of days [satisfied] (Job 42:16-17)." Even though Job's trials comprise the bulk of the Book of Job, *his problems continued only a few months; whereas he was blessed many years, both before and after that traumatic event.* So, let not Job's inaccurate words hinder your trust in God's Word. The Bible is an inspired account of *BOTH* God's and men's words—*and some of the men's words were outright lies. NO ONE Scripture passage represents ALL of the Bible!* So, we have to study, to show ourselves approved unto God (2 Timothy 2:15). Obviously, John Calvin did little *HONEST* Bible studying. *He just did a lot of LYING!*

Remember, Calvin basically called God a liar in his commentary on Exodus 32:33. Even though he tried to hide behind that accommodation ploy, *in essence John Calvin accused God Who cannot lie of lying—for, Moses' words were inspired by the Holy Spirit*—Who Himself is *GOD* (Acts 5:3-4). Moreover, because of Calvin's *RIGID* stance that names cannot be blotted out of the Book of Life, *we would have to conclude that Calvin would even accuse our Savior of lying*—Who said in Revelation 3:5: *"I WILL NOT BLOT THE NAME OF ANY OVERCOMER FROM THE BOOK OF LIFE." If names cannot be blotted out of the Book of Life ANYWAY, the Lord's promise was meaningless.* For, *He promised that over-comers would not be blotted out of the Book of Life.* That has to mean that non-over-comers will be blotted out. *Calvin lied!*

John Calvin published no commentary on the Book of Revelation—*but the man did refer to a few passages of Revelation in his Institutes.* However, Revelation 3:5 was *NOT ONE OF THEM.* Obviously then, *that Scripture passage was one of those Calvin dealt with BY refusing to deal with it.* He just skipped over it. But, nobody can *RIGHTLY DIVIDE* God's Word like that! By his inaction, Calvin revealed his bias against *ANY* Scripture passage that exposes and destroys his theology. Calvin opted to lie against God, and even *IMPLY THAT GOD IS A LIAR*, rather than admit that he himself just might be wrong.

A fifth Scripture passage that agrees with the other four, but *DISAGREES* with Calvin, is Revelation 22:19— which states in no uncertain terms: "And, if any man [including John Calvin] takes away *FROM* the words of the book of this prophecy, God will take his part *FROM* the Book of Life, out of the holy city, and out of [all the good] things, which are written in this book." *Although some Greek manuscripts substitute Tree of Life for Book of Life in that passage, it makes LITTLE difference.* For, if the Tree of Life is off-limits to one (as with Adam and Eve after they fell), neither is their name in the Book of Life. Revelation 2:7 says: "To him who overcomes, I will give to eat of the Tree of Life which is in the Paradise of God." Revelation 3:5 says over-comers' names will not be blotted out of the Book of Life. In other words, only over-comers are promised eternal access to the Tree of Life, *and their names eternally remaining in the Book of Life. Calvin opened wide the church doors to the devil!*

Believers who do not overcome will be blotted out of the Book of Life! That has to be referring to Christians running that race of Hebrews 12:1. Else, how can one be an overcomer? Overcome what? Unbelievers cannot be *over-comers—UNLESS they enter the Christian race.* The truth is that names which were once written in the Book of Life *CAN* be blotted out of it—if Christians fall away—which is actually prophesied to occur in the last days (1 Timothy 4:1). *Let us look at some passages that prove believers truly can depart from the Christian faith.*

39

Calvin's theology contends the very opposite. Christ addressed that issue in John 15:1-2 by clearly stating: "I am the True Vine; My Father is the husbandman [or farmer]. *EVERY* branch *IN ME* that bears no fruit, God takes away [severs it from the vine—Jesus Christ]: And every branch which bears fruit [by reason of abiding in Me], God prunes it; that it may bring forth more fruit." Some try to offset the truth of that passage by insisting that Jesus meant God would take fruitless believers on to heaven. Someone actually told me that to my face. I kid you not. That would mean heaven is *THE REWARD FOR A FRUITLESS LIFE.* Before a Christian reaches the point where he or she might *FALL AWAY AND BE LOST AGAIN,* God will actually kill them and take them on to heaven. *That is what the Lord MEANT by their removal; THEY SAY. But fruitlessness is more serious than that!*

That religious idea was spawned by Calvinism. *But, even that argument AGREES that people can fall away and be lost again*—God will kill them before they reach that point! John 15:6: "If a man abides not in Me, *he is cast out as a branch* [once attached, but then severed], *and is withered; and angels gather them and cast them into the FIRE, and they are burned." Does that sound to you like heaven? INSTEAD,* it is a picture of people who were once saved becoming lost once again and going to Hell! Galatians 5:2: "If you are circumcised, Christ will profit you nothing." Salvation being profitable, *if Christ becomes unprofitable to the Christian, that has to mean loss of salvation! One can be lost again after being born again!* Galatians 5:4: *"Christ HAS BECOME of no effect unto whoever tries to be justified by the law*—you have fallen from grace." *We are saved by grace through faith; so falling from grace has to mean losing one's salvation! You cannot fall from a place you have not been. There is no getting around that obvious Bible Truth!*

Chapter V

Calvin's lying and accusing III

I know of more than one respected Christian leader, who started out well, but then became deceived in some areas of doctrine—and then disseminated their errors in their published works. Eventually their doctrinal errors became *publicly exposed. And when that happened, the respect people had for the author was AUTOMATICALLY damaged—at least to some degree. Just one error tends to DULL the SHARP EDGE of their ministry.* We can still maintain some respect for those leaders, and continue to learn through their ministry. But thereafter, we tend to develop a cautious approach to any of their writings. If more than one *SERIOUS ERROR* surfaces, respect for that ministry suffers even more—*and we begin to LOSE FAITH IN BOTH THAT MINISTER AND THAT MINISTRY. Such response is not necessarily deliberate on our part.* Our trust having been *VIOLATED,* we *AUTOMATICALLY become suspicious of their teachings thereafter.*

In the case of John Calvin, however, we have found that the *ENTIRETY* of his belief *SYSTEM* is *DECEPTIVE. ALL FIVE TULIP TENETS OF CALVINISM ARE TOTALLY ERRONEOUS! Scripture exposes their demonic nature!*

John Calvin's *CESSATION-OF-MIRACLES doctrine* is one of the *LATTER-DAY HERESIES PAUL PROPHESIED ABOUT* in 1 Timothy 4:1. And that falsehood is just as *CENTRAL TO CALVINISM AS IS THE TULIP FARCE. Not only does John Calvin's CLAIM THAT GOD PURPOSELY REMOVED MIRACLES FROM THE CHURCH AFTER THE FIRST CENTURY COME SHORT OF BIBLICAL SUPPORT;*

the very opposite is clearly taught throughout the New Testament! Thus, every generation of Christians *during the church-age* is supposed to expect miracles—both in us—and through us to the unsaved. Calvin's Cessation doctrine has wrought *UNTOLD MISERY IN THE BODIES* of the members of the Body of Christ—*just as it did IN HIS OWN PHYSICAL BODY throughout his lifetime.* We will cover the *CESSATION DOCTRINE* in more depth in the following chapter—pointing out its *GREAT ERROR.*

But now, prepare for another *BUMPY RIDE* on John Calvin's off-track trail. *CALVINISM HAS RUTTY ROADS APLENTY!* Calvin implied that the apostle Paul lied just as had Moses, David, and Ezekiel—regarding names of the Elect being blotted out of the Book of Life. Whereas most English Bibles make Romans 9:3 imply that Paul said he *COULD WISH that he was accursed from Christ for the Jewish people,* the literal Greek says that *PAUL WAS* (formerly) *WISHING* that he would be accursed—*referring to his persecution of the church before he met Christ on the Damascus Road.* Prior to that experience, *Paul had ATTEMPTED TO STAMP OUT both the name of Jesus and His church* (Acts 26:9-11). After becoming a Christian, however, *Paul did not desire to be separated from Christ! How could that save anybody? Those Jews could be saved ONLY by coming into union with Christ; not by Paul's separation from Him!* So, in Romans 9:3, Paul must have spoken about his past disposition, not his current attitude. *That means Paul's statements had nothing to do with blotting names from the Book of Life.* Calvin missed the whole point of the words in Romans 9:3—*which appeared to be a threat to his theology.*

Now, moving on to Romans 7:9-11, where Paul said he was *ONCE ALIVE,* but sin revived and *HE DIED*; and Calvin's *LUDICROUS RESPONSE* to Paul's statements.

42

Paul's words taken literally would question Calvin's Total Depravity doctrine—so Calvin tried to disarm that Bible Truth. Although Paul clearly said *HE HAD ONCE BEEN ALIVE, BUT THEN DIED*, Calvin said it had *ONLY SEEMED TO PAUL* that he had at one time been *ALIVE*. The apostle had been *DECEIVED* about that, for it was impossible. Now, had Paul made that comment while he was *STILL* Saul of Tarsus, he might have been deceived about him being alive in those days. But Saul of Tarsus did not pen that passage. *THE APOSTLE PAUL WROTE IT BY HOLY SPIRIT INSPIRATION! Calvin accusing Paul of lying was an indirect accusation of the Holy Spirit! If Calvin had been right, Paul would have said that before being born again he had thought that he was alive; but after getting saved, he came to realize that he had been deceived while lost. But, Calvin was the deceived one!*

In Romans 7:9-11, Paul, by Holy Spirit inspiration, wrote: "I was alive once *WITHOUT THE LAW* [obviously referring to himself *BEFORE* he had reached the age of accountability]. But when the commandment came [as he began to learn the law as a Jewish boy], sin revived, and I died. That commandment, which was [supposed] to produce life, instead produced death. For sin, taking occasion by the commandment, deceived me, and by it killed me." Calvin said that *WAS A DELUSION* in Paul's mind. *John Calvin accused the apostle Paul, who wrote by Holy Spirit inspiration, of being DELUDED!*

Paul's words *THREATENED* Calvin's Total Depravity Doctrine: *Calvin right? Paul wrong?* The Greek/English New Testament wording puts that subject in a *BRAND NEW BIBLICAL LIGHT.* I first noticed that light in Jude 12—The King James Version: "False brothers are spots in your love-feasts, while they feast with you *WITHOUT GODLY FEAR; SERVING ONLY THEMSELVES. They are clouds without water—moved about by the winds—late autumn trees, without fruit—TWICE DEAD; PULLED UP BY THEIR ROOTS."* Now the *LITERAL GREEK: "HAVING DIED TWICE."* and *"HAVING BEEN UPROOTED." TWICE DEAD DOES NOT reveal the Bible Reality HAVING DIED TWICE does. That same truth can be seen with HAVING BEEN UPROOTED. They were not two times dead in the present; but were once dead, then made alive, and then became dead again—having died two times. If you have been DEAD two times, you have been ALIVE two times!* Not *"PULLED UP BY THE ROOTS"* presently: but rather, *"HAVING BEEN UPROOTED."* All of that had happened *IN THE PAST. That blasts the Total Depravity doctrine!*

Obviously, the impostors had never *DIED* physically even once. So, some other part of their being had died; and that *TWO TIMES*. So, it must have been their inner man—their spirit—that had died *TWO TIMES*. And that perfectly *AGREES* with Paul's words in Romans seven. *Saul of Tarsus had started out alive as a child, but at a certain age he sinned—and DIED spiritually. When Paul was born again he was made ALIVE once again.* Those in Jude had the same experience as Paul—except that they had later fallen away from the faith, and were lost again. How else could they have died twice? When they sinned the first time, they *DIED* their first death. After being born again, they were once again alive in Christ. Sometime later they fell away, *DYING A SECOND TIME*. That was when they were *UPROOTED*. Therefore, those men had to have been Christians at one time. A person cannot die without once having been alive. And, *DYING TWICE* necessitates that one has been *ALIVE TWICE*.

Remember, we are told in John 15:2: *"Every branch [believer] in Me that does not bear fruit God takes away [removes]."* That obviously speaks of one who has been

44

born again, and has come into union with Christ—has become a *BRANCH* in Christ, the True Vine—but later, gets severed from Christ and is lost again. That person has died twice! In John 15:6, the Lord further warned: "If anyone does not abide in Me, then he is cast out as a branch, and is *WITHERED*; and *THEY* [angels] gather them up, and they throw them into the *FIRE*, and they are burned." *That must be referring to people who have been BORN AGAIN and baptized into Christ by the Holy Spirit* (1 Corinthians 12:13). They had been Christians! Nobody can *BE SEVERED FROM A VINE* he or she was *NOT* attached to! Nobody can *DIE*, who was not already *ALIVE*. And, one cannot *DIE TWICE* who has not *LIVED TWICE*. Calvin deliberately ignored those Bible Truths!

Another clear case is found in 1 Timothy 5:6, where Paul wrote: "*[A Christian widow who is being supported by the church, but]* is living in pleasure, is *DEAD WHILE SHE LIVES*." Just as in Jude 12, the *LITERAL* Greek in that passage says she "*HAS DIED* [while] living." *If that woman HAD DIED, then she HAD BEEN ALIVE.* And, *if that woman was a widow, she was obviously an adult believer.* And, just like the guys in Jude 12, that widow had not died *physically*, but *spiritually*. Thus, biblically speaking, that woman had forfeited her salvation.

Calvin claimed that Jude 12 only meant that those men were not just dead, but *REALLY DEAD*. Jude used hyperbole—exaggeration! Calvin also said of the widow in 1 Timothy 5:6 that, "*she was merely non-productive. Not being useful she was as good as dead. Paul did not mean she lost her salvation.*" (*Calvin's interpretation*)

John Calvin never let the Bible get in the way of his theology. *IF a passage SEEMED to support his doctrinal view, he STUCK WITH the way it was written.* However,

IF a passage *SEEMED* that it might possibly expose the *ERRONEOUS* nature of his doctrinal view, *he hesitated not to either IGNORE it, DISTORT it, or outright DENY it.* John Calvin was a *LIAR, HERETIC,* and *BLASPHEMER!* How can anyone believe anything he wrote? His entire theological system is a *DECEPTIVE DEVILISH TRAP!*

Calvin ACCUSING PAUL OF BEING DECEIVED about his having been ALIVE as a child, and CONFUSED over the possibility of the ELECT being BLOTTED OUT of the Book of Life, implies that Calvin thought he knew more about those things than did Paul. *What ARROGANCE!*

Remember the Prodigal Son? *After that younger boy had obtained HIS PART of the family inheritance, he left home; then proceeded to waste his money, until he was FLAT BROKE. The lad eventually CAME TO HIMSELF— wised up—then returned home with A MORE HUMBLE ATTITUDE. When he showed up his father received him joyfully: "This my son, WAS DEAD, but is ALIVE AGAIN. He was LOST, but now he is FOUND (Luke 15:24)." The elder son, hearing that a party was being thrown for his kid brother, became angry, and refused to participate in the festivities.* The father came out to the elder sibling, and pleaded with him: "It was right to make merry and be glad; for your brother was *DEAD*, and is now *ALIVE* again; he was *LOST*, and is *FOUND* (Luke 15:32)."

The father not saying such about *BOTH* of his sons, the younger was obviously the one who had been alive, then died, then lived again—Not bodily, but spiritually!

Calvin said NOTHING about that young man DYING, then becoming ALIVE again. Instead, he said the family THOUGHT the young man had been lost geographically. (Duh!) On John Calvin's part, that was not ignorance; it was outright dishonesty. *LYING JOHN CALVIN!*

Genesis 2:7 tells us that when God *BREATHED* into Adam he became a *LIVING SOUL*. In Genesis 2:17, God warned Adam that if he sinned by eating the forbidden fruit, he would *DIE*. That had to mean spiritual death: Adam lived physically 930 years. Paul said that he was *ALIVE* until he sinned—at which time he died. And the men in Jude 12 had died twice. The type of widow Paul mentioned in 1 Timothy 5:6 had died while living. The Prodigal died as an adult, but became alive again when he repented. In order to maintain his doctrines, Calvin either ignored, denied, or distorted all those cases.

The Lord Himself agreed with Paul's words when He said in Matthew 19:14: *"Let those LITTLE children come to Me, and forbid them not; for of such is the Kingdom of heaven."* Mark 10:14-15 records the same, except with the addition: "Whosoever does not receive the Kingdom of God as a little child will by no means enter therein." Luke 18:15: "They even brought infants to Jesus, and He said the same of *INFANTS! They are of the Kingdom.*"

Infants could neither have sinned, nor accepted the Lord as Savior, at their tender age. Yet, Jesus said the Kingdom of God is *MADE UP OF SUCH*. Therefore, *Paul was ALIVE as a little child!* That means *innocent babies who are destroyed by ABORTION, or any other tragedy, immediately become heaven's residents.* Jesus said so!

Hosea 13:1 also agrees with Romans 7:9-11. "When Ephraim spoke, trembling, he exalted himself in Israel; but when he offended in Baal he died." Although Hosea spoke of a *TRIBE*, not an individual, the principle is the same. Some say the Jude 12 men had not been saved. But, Jude compared them to the angels that fell. *Those angels HAD NOT ALWAYS BEEN FALLEN angels! Jude ALSO COMPARED THOSE MEN WHO HAD DIED TWICE* to Balaam; who had not always been a *FALSE* prophet. *Surely, the Early church elders would not have granted church membership to men they KNEW had never been born again.* Thus, *they must have ONCE been believers, but later fell from the Christian faith—and then became the devil's tools to deceive other believers in the church.*

Two primary points in this chapter: One, *we human beings begin our earthly existence alive, both physically and spiritually—as Paul made it clear in Romans seven.* Second, John Calvin lied again, and again, in all of his dealings with those passages we have *STUDIED* in this section of *THIS* book. *Calvin avoided the clear message of each of those Scripture passages, while attempting to use some of them to prove doctrines which those verses did not even mention.* Thus, Calvin read into Scripture things which were not there. Moreover, he implied that some Holy-Spirit-Inspired Bible authors were deceived; insinuating that he knew more biblical truth than they did. *What arrogance of that devil's mouthpiece!*

If some of the Bible writers were mistaken in some of the Scriptures they penned, how are we supposed to know which ones we can trust just as they are written, *and which ones we must consult John Calvin about???*

Faith comes NOT through Calvinism, but BY hearing God's Inspired Word! So measure Calvin's doctrines by that faith-producing Holy-Spirit-Inspired Word of God.

Next, we will *CONTRAST* Calvin's Cessation doctrine with what the Bible actually teaches about *MIRACLES: MOST ENLIGHTENING AND LIBERATING!*

Chapter VI

Calvin's Demonic Cessation doctrine

When you *DECIDE* to study the Scriptures with an *HONEST HEART AND MIND,* you will learn Bible Truth regarding whatever subject is on your heart and mind. Of course, nobody can learn all there is to know about any Bible subject in just one lifetime—*for Bible Truth is inexhaustible.* You can, however, *establish inside you a solid Bible foundation*, on which you can build your life successfully. *That is the truth I discovered in the Lord's words in* Luke 6:46-49. *It is simple and to the point.*

However, in studying the Bible, a common mistake people make is *being overly concerned about the correct interpretation of Scripture.* But, I have learned that God did not send His Word to be interpreted, but instead to be *OBEYED!* One of John Calvin's worst mistakes was *INTERPRETING* Scripture. Repeatedly, in Calvin's *Bible Commentaries* and *"Institutes of the Christian Religion," that theologian contended that his interpretations were the correct ones—and that everybody else MUST accept HIS INTERPRETATIONS*—even when his interpretations were diametrically opposed to God's *WRITTEN* Word!

And, not in just one or two isolated cases, but in all Calvin was famous for. *Calvinism OPPOSES THE CORE TRUTHS of Scripture. Fighting against Roman Catholic ERRORS, Calvin replaced them with WORSE errors—all the while claiming HIS THEOLOGY WAS THE CORRECT INTERPRETATION OF THE BIBLE. However, rather than seeking for the correct Bible interpretation, we need our spiritual EYES opened to Bible Truth* (Ephesians 1:18). *The Bible is its own interpretation. But, most had rather interpret the Bible than obey it!* (John Calvin exactly!)

Interpreting Scripture always invites error! Actually, *there is only ONE correct interpretation of Bible Truth— what God's Word plainly says!* If some Bible passages seem to be obscure to you (And, such is just as true in my case as it is with anybody else.), put your inquiries about such things on your wait-for-God-to-reveal-His-truth-about-them shelf, so to speak, and then obey the Scriptures you do understand. I have one pastor friend whom I have heard many times confess that: "It is not those Scriptures I *DO NOT* understand that bother me, but those I *DO* understand." Obviously, *he means that he knows he is responsible to obey the scriptural truths he has been shown,* whereas God might cut him some slack on the ones he still has honest questions about.

Why have I begun this chapter by talking about the *ERRONEOUS CONCEPT* that God's Written Word needs to be interpreted? Because, *John Calvin built his entire theological system on that unbiblical practice. What the Bible plainly teaches meant nothing to John Calvin. His UNIQUE interpretations took the place of the very Word of God! Then he proudly pushed his personal position!*

Check out this RIDICULOUS COMMENT BY Calvin on Genesis 4:7; *where God warned Cain that sin sought to enslave him*—then commanded Cain to *RULE* over sin. *CALVIN CONTENDED THAT GOD DID NOT MEAN THAT CAIN SHOULD RULE OVER SIN.* That rendering would jeopardize Calvin's Total Depravity doctrine. No matter the actual wording of Genesis 4:7, *God could NOT have meant Cain should rule over sin—but INSTEAD over his brother Abel!* (Calvin's words!) If the plain truth of any passage came short of *SUPPORTING* Calvin's theology, *he would adjust the language until it DID SUPPORT his theology. Calvin even went so far as to imply that what God Himself said was not really true!* (What arrogance!)

Calvin's EDUCATED (????) INTERPRETATIONS were NOT ONLY erroneous in themselves, but they often even suggested that God's Word AS WRITTEN did not really present the truth—while Calvin had INSIDE information on it by his understanding of God's SECRET (???) WILL!

Calvinism is merely a collection of human opinions. *God backs NO human opinion! God supports HIS WORD ALONE! CALVINISM HAS NO BIBLE-BACKING. IT ONLY HAS PEOPLE-SUPPORT. And that by DECEIVED people!*

This chapter destroys John Calvin's claim that God *CEASED TO WORK MIRACLES; AND EVEN CEASED TO DESIRE TO PERFORM MIRACLES, BEYOND THE FIRST CENTURY. JOHN CALVIN PEDDLED CESSATIONISM AS OFFICIAL CHURCH DOCTRINE—claiming miracles were no longer needed, because—ALTHOUGH THE CHURCH HAD BEEN ESTABLISHED UPON MIRACLES, THE NEW TESTAMENT BOOKS HAD REPLACED MIRACLES. And that DEMONIC DOCTRINE prevails in most churches to this day—*deceiving and destroying countless lives.

Christ, however, said that miracles are supposed to continue occurring in every generation—*until He comes back again!* I have written two books on the subject of sickness and healing. However, since those books were published, *the Holy Spirit has revealed to me even more essential Bible Truth on divine healing.* I share with you some of those *HEALING EXTRAS* in this chapter. You can find out more about the healing books and others on this website: www.livingwayfellowshiponline.org.

Biblical REVELATION on DIVINE HEALING is beyond dispute. The more we *HONESTLY* study the Scriptures on miracle-healing, the more we find that *God's will for us believers is PERFECT HEALTH. With that Bible Truth established inside us, we need NOT be concerned about CORRECT Bible interpretation regarding our health.* We already have it! Once again, *THE PRIMARY KEY is to be honest with God's Word.* Without consulting Scripture, *Calvin said that God planned that miracles would cease AFTER the first century. By the time John, THE LAST of the original twelve apostles, died, the need for miracles no longer existed—because the church was established, and Scripture was enough to persuade people to repent without the aid of miracles—JOHN CALVIN'S SUPERIOR (actually demonic) INTERPRETATION!*

He arrived at THAT conclusion, NOT after thoroughly and honestly studying the Scriptures, but BY observing his own physical circumstances. John Calvin judged by sense information, not scriptural revelation. In my first healing volume, I either spelled out or listed *over seven hundred different Scripture passages which deal either directly or indirectly with the sickness/healing subject.*

On the other hand, *Calvin tackled only one passage that mentions DIVINE HEALING*—James 5:14. He could hardly dismiss the truth of that Scripture. However, he concluded that the command for sick Christians to call for church elders to *PRAY* for their miraculous healing was valid only for believers during the early days of the church. It was only temporary—*not a blessing believers can expect during the entire church-age.* Again Calvin's *SUPERIOR* (but in reality, demonic) *INTERPRETATION!*

Do you know how many *biblical principles* that man violated in forming that *UNBIBLICAL* conclusion? First, *IN THE MOUTH OF TWO OR THREE WITNESSES MUST EVERY WORD BE ESTABLISHED. NO EXCEPTIONS!* So, *it is unbiblical to FOUND any theological doctrine on one passage alone—and especially if that passage has been taken out of context, or perverted IN ANY WAY.* In John Calvin's case, *he built his doctrine, NOT on what* James 5:14 *DID say, but on what it DID NOT say. Nowhere did James indicate, or even hint, that what he commanded was NOT a permanent church blessing.* Therefore, *John Calvin built his SICK THEOLOGY on no Scripture at all!* Rather, he injected into Scripture his own speculation; which violated still *ANOTHER biblical principle*—Do not add to or take away from the message of any Scripture passage. Those two obvious infractions encompass the violation of still another biblical principle—it also being in the epistle of James: *"LIE NOT AGAINST THE TRUTH* (James 3:14)!" John Calvin said that James 5:14 does not express God's will for believers today. Instead, *God sometimes wants believers to be sick for His glory!* (???)

Doing the devil service, Calvin deliberately *SKIPPED OVER* the Scripture passages that prove divine healing *IS* a New Testament blessing for the entire church-age. Upon *DISMISSING* them, *Calvin proceeded to construct his SPECULATION into a theological system that denies the miraculous—then expected the church to believe HIS THEOLOGY, which has NO BIBLE SUPPORT whatever!*

In Luke 11:23, the Lord said that those who are not with Him are *AGAINST* Him; and that those who do not gather with Him *SCATTER. That applies to every aspect of Christ's ministry—NOT just to the forgiveness-of-sins part. Calvin's insistence that the miracle-ministry Jesus established later ceased fits the warning in* Luke 11:23. *The DEMONIC DOCTRINES inhabiting Calvin's writings have done a lot of SCATTERING over five centuries.* The man will be held accountable for both his mishandling of Scripture, and *THE DESTRUCTIVE EFFECTS OF HIS UNGODLY DOCTRINES* on multitudes of believers *AND* non-believers alike over the past five hundred years!

To convince himself that his theology was the correct interpretation of Scripture, Calvin had to either IGNORE, DENY, or otherwise PERVERT many Scripture passages that not only EXPOSE his doctrines as being thoroughly demonic, but explicitly teach the VERY OPPOSITE of his anti-miracle theology. In his "Institutes of the Christian Religion" Calvin mentioned numerous Scriptures that I included in my healing books; but *WOULD EMPHASIZE* what those passages said about *SIN*, and totally ignore *ALL* references to miracle-healing. According to Calvin, Isaiah 53:5, Matthew 8:16-17, Galatians 3:13, 1 Peter 2:24, etc. *illustrate ONLY SIN-SICKNESS, and ought not be seen as promises of physical healing.* Those authors used miracle-healings only as illustrations to promote the much greater blessing of soul-salvation. (???????)

Who says we have to choose BETWEEN forgiveness of sins and bodily healing? Jesus asked: *"Which one is easier to say to a man paralyzed in his body*: 'Your sins are forgiven' or 'Get up and walk!'?"* The truth is, *Jesus healed our bodies in the very same sacrifice that saved us from sin!* (You would definitely profit by reading my two books on Divine healing.) When commenting upon Galatians 3:13, Calvin ignored the fact that the *CURSE* of the law included sickness and disease of every kind. On the cross, *Jesus became a curse to deliver us FROM THE CURSE.* Deuteronomy 28:15-68 lists many bodily ailments—calling them all *CURSES.* (The word curse in Hebrew *MEANS TO LOWER ONE TO A LESSER STATE. That should shake some church members awake!*)

In Calvin's Institutes, there is *NO* reference to John 14:12, where Christ promised: "Truly, truly, I say unto you that he who believes in Me will do the same works that I do." And, in his Bible Commentary on that verse, *Calvin studiously avoided the subject of the miraculous!*

What *KIND* of works did Christ do? Miraculous works! John 14:12 completely destroys John Calvin's demonic theology. Another passage is Matthew 28:18-20; which Calvin mentioned more than one time, but deliberately ignored the fact that the passage teaches Jesus Christ expects believers to *PERPETUATE* His miracle-ministry until He comes back—*Commanding Christians to make disciples of all the nations, and then teach them to obey all those things He commanded that first generation of believers to do!* Which means our Lord *EXPECTS* us to heal the sick, cast out demons, raise the dead, cleanse lepers, etc. That agrees with 1 John 2:6—which states: "He who says that he *ABIDES* in Him [in Christ] ought himself also to walk *JUST AS HE* [Christ] walked." *That has to include performing miracles just as the Lord did; and cannot be RESTRICTED to just a MORAL Gospel. At best, Calvin's theology is little more than a moral code— whereas Christ commanded Christians to continue His SUPERNATURAL ministry to the end of the present age.*

Matthew 24:14 *alone SETTLES the miracle-question*: "This Gospel of the Kingdom will be preached in all the world for a witness unto all nations—and then the end will come." The eye-opening word in this verse is *THIS*: *THIS GOSPEL. Which Gospel? John Calvin's powerless THEOLOGY, or the GOOD NEWS that Jesus PREACHED AND DEMONSTRATED BY MIRACULOUSLY healing the sick,* casting out demons, etc.? Our Lord was evidently referring to the Gospel *HE* preached; not to some other message masquerading as the real Gospel that delivers from *ALL* detrimental circumstances! *Christ prophesied that the SAME Gospel which He preached while He was on earth will be preached on earth in OUR day. And His Gospel was a miracle-producing Gospel—Which means THAT THE SAME MIRACLE-WORKING MINISTRY THAT JESUS WALKED IN ought to be prominent in OUR day!*

John Calvin taught that God wants us to accept our painful ailments as His will for our lives—no questions asked. That doctrine is obviously *DEMONIC*, because it directly *OPPOSES* the Scriptures we have covered thus far. *Do you realize that Satan himself is behind all such theological delusions? God would NEVER contradict His own Word! John Calvin did all the contradicting—being driven by the chief-contradictor—the devil himself.*

MAYBE WITHOUT REALIZING IT JOHN CALVIN WAS IN LEAGUE WITH THE DEVIL. HOW DARE I SAY SUCH ABOUT THAT HIGHLY-RESPECTED THEOLOGIAN? Did Jesus not say the devil is the father of lies (John 8:44)? And, do not those Scriptures we have dealt with clearly teach the very opposite of John Calvin's doctrine on the subject? That necessarily means that John Calvin LIED when he contended that GOD PURPOSELY WITHDREW HIS MIRACLES from the church AFTER the first century! Lying about anything God *SAID* about anything makes one the devil's *ACCOMPLICE.* John Calvin, *on that and many other vital issues, was a mouthpiece for the devil!*

Calvin not being able to offer one Scripture passage to prove his doctrines is further proof that he lied. How could Calvin expect anyone to *TRUST HIS BARE WORD* on miracle-cessation—*he having no Bible proof to back his theological arguments*—while passage after passage loudly screams the opposite of his Cessation theology? Yet, *many people actually prefer lies over Bible Truth!*

Christ also said that *HIS GOSPEL* "Will be preached to *ALL NATIONS* by the end of this age." Those original apostles *NEVER PREACHED* in *Australia, the Americas, southern Africa, China, Russia, the islands of the seas,* or, *above the Arctic Circle*—in other words, to the *ENDS* of the earth—*as Jesus Christ commanded them to do in*

56

Acts 1:8. *That did not happen in the first century!* Thus, miracle-ministry being supposed to continue until the earth's ends are reached, *miracle-ministry is supposed to continue to our day and beyond—because the earth's ends have not yet been reached—which is definite proof that God did not plan for His miracle-works to cease!*

Christ's COMMANDS in Mark 16:15 *were essentially the same as in* Matthew 28:18-20; *plus His prophecy in* Matthew 24:14. In Mark 16:15, *Christ commanded His disciples to go into all the world.* Jesus surely knew the original twelve would not live long enough to evangelize the entire globe. Therefore, *His Gospel command MUST have encompassed the entire church-age*—those twelve apostles being only the first generation of Christians to whom that commission was given. However,...

Even to this day preachers will talk about *the Great Commission, BUT* delete the miraculous portion of that commission. *WHY do they DENY the miraculous, which Jesus Christ both promised and commanded? Because they are cowards when it comes to preaching the whole Gospel message. But they will pay for their cowardice!*

Luke 19:13 adds to *THE LIST* of Scripture passages that address that issue—*all being in TOTAL agreement with each other, but in total disagreement with Calvin's Miracle-Cessation doctrine.* A king went searching for a kingdom and *promised to return.* Before he left, *he gave his servants some currency to work with WHILE he was gone—commanding them: "DO BUSINESS WITH THESE UNTIL I RETURN." That illustrated what Christ expects of us Christians during the entire time He is absent from the earth; until His return. What kind of CURRENCY did Christ GIVE the church TO USE during His absence?* On the Day of Pentecost, He *BAPTIZED* Christians with the Holy Spirit

AND all of His supernatural gifts! That was the *POINT* of His parable in Luke chapter 19. *And that means God has expected Christians to perform miracles from the Day of Pentecost to the present day.* The Lord *said He would be with us ALL THE DAYS until the end of this age.* So, *there have been NO HEAVEN-PLANNED BREAKS from the miraculous—*Just *CALVIN-PLANNED BREAKS and DEVIL-PLANNED BREAKS!*

Moreover, Romans 11:29 *says in the Greek/English Interlinear New Testament: "The GIFTS and CALLING of God are without repentance." That means God will NOT change His mind about either the GIFTS or CALLING He has once for all invested in the church. The Greek word for gifts is charismata—SUPERNATURAL GRACE GIFTS.* The Greek word rendered without repentance signifies being irrevocable—*INCAPABLE OF BEING RECALLED!*

God not only *WILL NOT* recall the charismata—Holy Spirit gifts—*He CANNOT RECALL those gifts! He having given His Word, He CANNOT GO BACK on it.* What does that suggest in relation to Calvin's Cessation theory? *It PROVES that it is a demonic attack on the church!* And, the devil enlisted John Calvin to spearhead the attack!

First Corinthians 12:4-28, plus Ephesians 4:11-16, *agree that GOD HAS ESTABLISHED THE CHARISMATA within the church.* Romans 12:6-8 says the same about the charismata. *God HAVING INVESTED spiritual gifts in His church, they CANNOT BE REVOKED BEFORE the Lord returns.* Calvin—*a deceived, deceiving, hypocrite!*

Even the written works of the Early Church Fathers *prove John Calvin wrong—testifying that into the fourth century miracles continued to occur through people who obeyed God—*both men and women—even children!

58

Calvin reaped a harvest of curses from his very own theology. Believing that WHATEVER befalls us has to be God's will for us, the devil used Calvin's OWN doctrines to bring upon him MANY painful physical ailments. His very own theology opened that door to the devil. Then, *Calvin had the audacity to COMPLAIN ABOUT his many pains.* Edwin H. Palmer, one modern staunch Calvinist author, praised John Calvin for bearing great suffering in his service to God. (But, to *WHICH* god? Satan is the god of this world system, who steals, kills and destroys with sickness, disease, poverty, etc. Jesus Christ came that we might have life, and have it during our time on earth; not just after our body dies.) In Palmer's lauding of Calvin, he listed more physical ailments than I have ever heard of anyone bearing at any one time; let alone throughout *MOST OF HIS LIFE.* Palmer said Calvin had *serious headaches, troubles of the trachea, pains in his side, his lungs bleeding when he preached extra hard, pleurisy attacks, and consumption (tuberculosis) at the age of fifty-one. Calvin had a bad case of hemorrhoids, fever often, gallstones, kidney stones, stomach cramps, intestinal influenza, and arthritis.* Calvin once wrote in a letter that his condition was a constant struggle with *DEATH. And Palmer called Calvin a hero for bearing all of that demonic stuff! The devil must chuckle.*

John Calvin suffered all of that because of his own stupidity. That may sound harsh, but the man brought all of that upon himself through *HIS OWN* unscriptural theology. Had he been honest with the Bible, *instead of stubbornly holding onto his demented doctrines,* Calvin would have known that Satan is the author of sickness (Acts 10:38), and would have gained *FAITH* to resist it (Romans 10:17; James 4:7; 1 Peter 5:8-9). I *CONDEMN* nobody for suffering sickness. But I will say that *many Christians actually HELP the devil make and keep them*

59

sick by their unscriptural theology. To *ACCEPT* sickness as God's will for the faithful Christian is *a mere excuse for NOT TRUSTING GOD to keep His promises in* James 5:14-16, etc. *Christ healed every sickness on the cross. Divine healing is a CURRENT New Covenant blessing!!!*

Calvinists get all bent out of shape if anyone dares to question their theology. But if Calvinism truly is the *CORRECT BIBLE INTERPRETATION, WHY do they have to get upset when Calvinism is challenged?* They betray their own doubts and insecurities by such action.

Christ said His Truth will set us free—if we get His Truth down inside us. And it is OUR choice; contrary to Calvin's doctrine of Irresistible Grace—which claims no one has a choice—God chooses FOR us. Scripture says, on the other hand, that *we will give an account to God for every CHOICE WE MAKE.* Moreover,...

Limited Atonement is a demonic Calvinist *HERESY:* In Leviticus chapter sixteen, Moses instructed Aaron to sacrifice *TWO GOATS* to God on the Day of Atonement. *One goat was killed and placed on the altar—portraying Christ's body on the cross.* Then, *Aaron laid his hands on the head of the SECOND goat; confessing over it ALL the sins of the ENTIRE NATION of Israel—then releasing that live goat into the wilderness—portraying our Lord's SPIRIT descending into Hell. That LIVE goat carried ALL OF THE SINS of the ENTIRE nation of Israel.* Aaron did not curse the second goat with the sins of only *PART* of Israel, but *WITH ALL* of the sins of *ALL* Israel. *The Day of Atonement was a TYPE of Christ—So He had to fulfill that type in His sacrifice. If the type of Christ dealt with ALL the sins of Israel, then Christ bore EVERY sin of the ENTIRE WORLD—* Just as John 1:29 states! So, Limited Atonement is one more demonic Calvinist falsehood!

Chapter VII

Divine attributes and the Last Adam

In his religious *ZEAL* to combat Roman Catholicism and *RESTORE THE GENUINE CHRISTIAN FAITH*, John Calvin *OVERLOOKED TWO MORE BIBLE TRUTHS that expose his replacement religion as being just as bad as, or worse than, Roman Catholicism. The first Bible Truth is the reality that GOD'S PERSONALITY IS PERPETUAL. HIS REDEMPTIVE TITLES are proof of that Bible Truth! Since God does not change* (Malachi 3:6), *His character remains the same. That second Bible Truth is connected to Christ becoming the Last Adam on the cross. We will investigate BOTH Bible Realities—beginning with God's UNCHANGING REDEMPTIVE TITLES—then ferreting out the Bible Truth about the LAST ADAM on the cross.*

God's name JEHOVAH is combined with redemptive titles that reveal not only His REDEMPTIVE ACTIVITIES, but His REDEMPTIVE CHARACTER. We will first look at what His name *JEHOVAH*, or *YAHWEH*, signifies.

JEHOVAH basically means the *ETERNAL ONE, THE SELF-EXISTENT ONE*, and the *IMMUTABLE ONE*—all of which prove that *JEHOVAH* does not, indeed *CANNOT*, change—but *remains the same from eternity to eternity.* Some prefer *YAHWEH*, but the more well-known title is *JEHOVAH*—appearing as *SUCH* in Exodus 6:3, Psalms 83:18, Isaiah 12:2 and 26:4 in the King James Version of the Bible. *JEHOVAH* also *OFTEN* appears as *LORD— ALL CAPITALS*—in that King James Version. When you see *LORD* in any Bible version, it is either *JEHOVAH* or *YAHWEH*. And remember; neither the term *JEHOVAH*, nor any connected redemptive title will ever *CHANGE!*

One combination is Jehovah-Tsidkenu—the *LORD OUR RIGHTEOUSNESS*—Jeremiah 23:6, and 33:16, in the *KJV*. *JEHOVAH HIMSELF* is our righteousness! But, how did that happen? "God made Jesus, Who knew no sin, to become sin for us, so that we might become *THE RIGHTEOUSNESS of God in Him* (2 Corinthians 5:21)." *Jesus Christ purchased that blessing for us on the cross —by which He connected those who believe to Jehovah-Tsidkenu—THE LORD OUR RIGHTEOUSNESS. In this and ALL CASES, WHO GOD IS DETERMINES WHAT HE DOES. And since God IS always the SAME, then He will obviously keep ACTING the SAME! God will ALWAYS be THE LORD OUR RIGHTEOUSNESS—to all believers.*

Jehovah-Mekaddishkem *is another combination that means The LORD is our SANCTIFIER*—found in Exodus 31:13. Hebrews 2:11: "*HE WHO SANCTIFIES* and those who are being sanctified are all of One [God *in Christ*]." "Christ became for us wisdom, and righteousness, and *SANCTIFICATION* (1 Corinthians 1:30)." *Jesus paid the cross-price to SANCTIFY everyone who believes for that cross-benefit.* But, *it was offered to us because of God's UNCHANGING SANCTIFYING CHARACTER!*

Of course, the *BEST-KNOWN JEHOVAH* redemptive title is *THE LORD IS OUR SHEPHERD*—Jehovah-Rohi— in Psalms 23:1. *Jesus is that GOOD SHEPHERD; as we see in* John 10:14: "*I am the GOOD SHEPHERD.*" *Jesus was called the SHEPHERD and Overseer of our souls in* 1 Peter 2:25. *He purchased all of God's redemptive-title blessings on the cross. SO, THE BLESSINGS ARE JUST AS UNCHANGING as is God's redemptive CHARACTER!*

Still another redemptive title is Jehovah-Nissi—The *LORD is our BANNER—VICTOR*—Exodus 17:15: "*Moses built an altar and called it THE-LORD-IS-MY-BANNER.*"

LORD there is *JEHOVAH. And Jesus Christ IS THAT BANNER*—Isaiah 11:10: "The root of Jessie [Jesus] will *STAND AS A BANNER* to the people." First Corinthians 15:57 proves Jesus Christ is that *BANNER—VICTORY*: "God always gives us the *VICTORY THROUGH* our Lord Jesus Christ." *That was paid for BY HIS BLOOD, which He shed upon that tree.* In Scripture, the word *BANNER* means more than a *FLAG. It stands for VICTORY.* True *VICTORY* comes *ONLY* through Jesus Christ. However, that victory is based on Jehovah's *BANNER-NATURE!*

Jehovah-Shammah—*THE LORD IS THERE, or THE LORD IS PRESENT.* Ezekiel 48:35: "*The name of the city* [Jerusalem] *will be called THE LORD IS THERE*; or *THE LORD IS PRESENT.*" Matthew 28:20 reveals that Christ also *FILLS* that *REDEMPTIVE ROLE*: "*I am WITH you* all the days *TO THE END OF THE AGE.*" For, "Jesus is the *SAME* yesterday, today and *FOREVER* (Hebrews 13:8)." And, God Himself has said: "*I WILL NEVER LEAVE YOU NOR FORSAKE YOU* (Hebrews 13:5-6)." He is present!

Jehovah-Shalom—*THE LORD IS OUR PEACE. The Hebrew word SHALOM includes PEACE, PROSPERITY, HEALTH, WHOLENESS, WELL-BEING.* "Gideon built an altar unto the Lord, and called it *THE-LORD-IS-PEACE* (Judges 6:24)." Again, *Jesus Christ paid the cross-price that provided that blessing for everyone who BELIEVES FOR IT*—Isaiah 53:5: "*By His bruise* [singular], *we are healed* [peace within our *BODY*]." Ephesians 2:14 *says Jesus Christ IS OUR PEACE.* Romans 15:33: "*THE GOD OF PEACE WILL BE WITH YOU* [believers]." *GOD ACTS OUT OF HIS UNCHANGING REDEMPTIVE CHARACTER.*

One more *Divine redemptive title is Jehovah-Jireh— THE-LORD-OUR-PROVIDER*—Genesis 22:14: "Abraham named that place *THE-LORD-WILL-PROVIDE—just as it is said to this very day: 'In the Mountain of the Lord, it will be provided.'" God's Redemptive ACTS are ALWAYS based upon His UNCHANGING REDEMPTIVE NATURE!*

And once again, *Jesus Christ was connected to that provision-blessing by becoming poor upon the cross—so that we Christians might be made RICH (richly supplied with everything that we need—2* Corinthians 8:9). Also Philippians 4:19: *"GOD WILL SUPPLY ALL YOUR NEED,* according to His riches in glory *BY JESUS CHRIST."*

Jehovah-Rapha—*THE LORD OUR HEALER: God will never back off from His divine-healing-activity, because HE IS THE HEALER.* Neither Father God nor Christ will ever *CHANGE—SO SAY* Malachi 3:6 and Hebrews 13:8. Exodus 15:26: *"I AM THE LORD WHO HEALS."* And, *IT IS "BY* Christ's bruise [singular] that *WE ARE HEALED* (Isaiah 53:5)." Matthew 8:16-17 says that *JESUS TOOK* our infirmities, and *BORE* our diseases, to fulfill Isaiah 53:5. First Peter 2:24: *"Himself BORE OUR SINS in His own body on the tree [cross], so that we, having died to sin, may live UNTO RIGHTEOUSNESS: by Whose bruise [singular] we were HEALED."* The *SAME* price was paid for our bodily healing as for the forgiveness of our sins!

"ALL OF GOD'S PROMISES IN CHRIST ARE YES AND AMEN (2 Corinthians 1:20)." Thus, Christ is connected to *ALL* of God's *UNCHANGING REDEMPTIVE TITLES.*

When John Calvin SPECULATED that God withdrew all miracle-ministries after the first century, he failed to take into account that all those miracle-ministries came out of GOD'S UNCHANGEABLE MIRACLE-CHARACTER. God cannot alter WHO HE IS, and WHO HE IS has been revealed in His redemption PLAN—and Christ's sacrifice on the cross to achieve God's redemption PLAN. Christ's DEPOSIT OF HIS SHED BLOOD upon the heavenly altar

(Hebrews 9:12) *is a GUARANTEE that EVERYTHING He wrought for us by His SHED BLOOD will ever be intact, cannot be altered, or lose its effectiveness. Therefore, all of those cross-blessings are as available today as when Christ's blood was first deposited up in heaven!!!!!*

Only one time was our Lord called the *LAST ADAM. Why the LAST* Adam, *and why was He called that only once?* (1 Corinthians 15:45-47) *Some authors mention that passage, but NONE understands what Paul taught there. Most call Jesus the second Adam—some the new Adam.* Now, *females being part of the human race, and Adam being HEAD of the human race, when our Savior BECAME the Last Adam on that cross, He represented males and females. But, in His resurrection, He became a life-giving Spirit* (1 Corinthians 15:45)—*and so is now neither male nor female*: *"In Christ, there is neither male nor female* (Galatians 3:28)" Resurrected believers will not procreate (Matthew 22:30). But now continuing,...

In 1 Corinthians 15:45, Adam is called *the first man Adam.* In the Greek, it is *protos* (first) *anthropos* (man) *Adam.* Genesis 2:7 says: *"The LORD formed Adam from the dust of the ground, and BREATHED into his nostrils the breath of LIFE; and the man BECAME a living soul."* First Corinthians 15:45 also tells us that the *Eschatos* (last) *Adam*—Jesus Christ—became a life-giving Spirit.

First Corinthians 15:47: *"The protos anthropos* (first man) *was made out of dust; but the deuteros anthropos* (second man) *was the Lord Jesus Christ from heaven.* Jesus Christ was *NEVER CALLED* the *SECOND ADAM:* Nor the *NEW ADAM. But He was designated the second man—the deuteros* (second) *anthropos* (man). And that happened after He had been the Last Adam for a short time—*on the cross and in Hades three days and nights.*

On that cross, our Savior became everything Adam had become through his *FALL*—sin and all its curses—achieving total redemption from sin and all the curses! "God has *MADE HIM* [Jesus] Who did no sin *TO BE SIN* for us; *that we might be made the righteousness of God IN HIM* (2 Corinthians 5:21)." *Our Lord BECOMING SIN was the primary part of His becoming the Last Adam on that cross.* John 1:29: "*Behold, the Lamb of God, WHO takes away the sin of the whole world.*" But what made it legal for Christ to take upon Himself the sins of this entire planet? God does not do things *HAPHAZARDLY*: He is obligated to *PLAY BY HIS OWN RULES*—which He laid down at man's creation, and authorization to have dominion on this earth. (I have a book telling all about God's rules governing *EARTHLY AUTHORITY*.)

But now let us consider more *sin-bearing* passages: Isaiah 53:4: "[Upon the cross] *CHRIST WAS WOUNDED FOR OUR TRANSGRESSIONS; AND WAS BRUISED FOR OUR INIQUITIES.*" Further sin-bearing revelation,...

Isaiah 53:6: "*The LORD has laid on Him* [Christ] *the iniquity of us all.*" That amounts to sinful Adam himself being laid on Christ on that cross—because, as we will shortly see, *the Bible actually EQUATES Adam with sin.* Therefore, *sin being laid upon Jesus was the very same as Adam being laid upon Him—and that happened only upon the cross.* Jesus Christ became the Last Adam on the cross—and remained the Last Adam *UNTIL He was made alive in Hades, then resurrected on the third day.* Thus, *Jesus was the Last Adam for only a SHORT time.*

Adam's race is equated with sin, unrighteousness, and lawlessness. In 2 Corinthians 6:14-15 *Paul asked:* "*What fellowship has righteousness with lawlessness? What communion has light* [us believers] *with darkness* [unbelievers]? *What agreement is there between Christ and the devil? And what part do BELIEVERS have with UNBELIEVERS?" Unbelievers are basically identified as unrighteousness, sin and lawlessness.* Thus, when the Savior *WAS MADE TO BE SIN* (2 Corinthians 5:21), He was made to be *ADAM—who was all of those things.*

"The one who commits SIN commits lawlessness. For SIN IS LAWLESSNESS (1 John 3:4)." SIN IS EQUATED WITH LAWLESSNESS! So, *SIN AND LAWLESSNESS are interchangeable terms. Thus, WHEN JESUS WAS MADE TO BE SIN, HE WAS MADE TO BE LAWLESSNESS.*

First John 5:17 *tells us UNRIGHTEOUSNESS IS SIN: Which makes sin and unrighteousness interchangeable terms—just like sin and lawlessness.* All three describe Adam in his fallen state—a sinner—and even sin itself. That has to mean that when Christ became sin on the cross He became Adam—the Last Adam—who was said to be sin, lawlessness, and unrighteousness. *So, Christ becoming sin was the same as Christ becoming Adam.*

But, *how did Adam become all sinners in the human race? Scripturally simple!* Genesis 14:20 says Abraham gave Melchizedek a *TITHE* of all. *THEN* Hebrews 7:9-10 says: "Levi who receives tithes *PAID TITHES* through Abraham. For, he [Levi] was in the *LOINS* [reproductive organs] of his great-grand-father Abraham on that day when Melchizedek met him [Abraham]."

Notice: Levi, Abraham's great-grand-son, was inside Abraham's physical body three generations before Levi was born! *That was based upon the SEED principle God built into plants, animals, and people—natural creation:* That means *the entire human race was INSIDE Adam's physical body in the form of reproductive seeds. EVERY HUMAN BEING DESCENDED FROM ADAM. Ponder this*:

How many acorns may be ON one oak tree? Many! But, how many OAK TREES are IN one acorn? An unlimited number! The same with Adam and the human race.

Moreover, Jesus *Christ did not become just PART of Adam, but ALL of Adam.* That means Jesus Christ died for the entire human race. Since we were in Adam, and Christ died for *US*, then Christ had to become Adam *IN ORDER FOR HIS SACRIFICE TO AFFECT US! By Christ becoming the Last Adam, He became all of us who were in Adam. That Bible Truth completely destroys Calvin's LIMITED ATONEMENT farce—which claims that Christ died only for a LIMITED number of people—THE ELECT.* So once again, Demonic Calvinism bites the dust!

NOT having been *FATHERED* by any man in Adam's race, *the Lord could not have become the Last Adam at either His conception or His birth—for even though Mary was His mother, GOD was His Father. Christ could only have become the Last Adam during His cross-sacrifice!*

Our Savior could *NOT* have redeemed us by bearing cross-sufferings as some Adam other than that original Adam. *The sin problem being IN Adam, and we being IN Adam, to solve our sin problem Jesus had to become the original Adam—where we humans were located!*

Hebrews 2:16: *"Jesus took not on Himself the nature of angels; but the Seed of Abraham."* Being born a Jew, *if Jesus had died only as a Jew, He would redeem only the Jews.* To die for *BOTH* Jew and Gentile—the whole human race—our Savior had to become *THE ORIGINAL SINNER—the one who held inside him the entire human race—*the fallen Adam. *So Jesus shed His blood for ALL humanity, not for just a limited number of people called the ELECT.* Calvinism—*A NOT-TOO-SMART theology!*

Chapter VIII

Calvin's erroneous foundation

In Calvin's "Institutes of the Christian Religion" and Bible Commentaries, *he could SPOT doctrines in certain Scripture passages that held not a ghost of proof of his doctrines—while deliberately denying the truths clearly exhibited in those passages. Did John Calvin come from some other planet? Was the man a genius? Did he have a gift of discernment which God granted to no one else? Or, was John Calvin a DEMONIC PLANT in the church? Was the devil ENABLED by John Calvin to INFILTRATE the church, and DESTROY it from within?* If you believe the Bible, *then the ANSWER to those last two questions is a resounding YES! Calvinism is AT ODDS WITH GOD AND HIS WORD. That is plain to all who WANT to see!*

You cannot believe Calvinism and Holy Scripture at the same time. No one can serve two masters (Matthew 6:24). We have to choose between *CALVINISM* and *THE BIBLE!* I have not read everything Calvin wrote; but his thousand-page Institutes and twenty-two-volume Bible Commentary set *contain enough information to provide one with a thorough understanding of Calvin's theology. I have READ Calvin's Institutes THREE TIMES* (portions of it *MORE*); *and SEARCHED his Bible Commentaries to get his views on ALL of the doctrines he PUSHED in his infamous theology.* Therefore, *I KNOW EXACTLY* where Calvin stood on all of the major Calvinist doctrines.

Moreover, *I have read the BIBLE from cover to cover more than once—finding it contradicts Calvin's brand of theology—proving that Calvinism EXALTS ITSELF above*

God's Word! I do not know *WHEN* John Calvin *BEGAN* to veer off track; but it is obvious that he was off track. Somewhere along the way, he developed a most bizarre concept of God's *SOVEREIGNTY*. To Calvin Sovereignty meant that *GOD IS IN COMPLETE CONTROL OF EVERY CREATED THING—ORCHESTRATING EVERY MOVE OF EVERY LIVING BEING—INANIMATE OBJECTS TOO!* No one can think, say or do anything which God, *BEFORE creation, had not PREDETERMINED WILL OCCUR. Even every occurrence in nature is SUPPOSEDLY under God's complete Sovereign control twenty-four sevens.*

Whereas that suggests that we ARE MERE ROBOTS, Calvin insisted that we ARE NOT ROBOTS! John Calvin controlling all sides of all arguments, he could win every one of them. Nobody could prove him wrong. But, that was in *JOHN CALVIN'S LITTLE THEOLOGICAL WORLD.* God made *THE REAL RULES* (not John Calvin); *and we will all be judged by GOD'S WRITTEN RULES. AMEN!*

Numbers 23:19: *"God is not man that he should LIE [People practice lying.]; neither the son of man [human] that He should repent:* Has He said, and will He not do what He said? Or, has He declared, and yet, not make His Words good?" Titus 1:2 states: *"GOD CANNOT LIE."* Hebrews 6:18: *"IT IS IMPOSSIBLE FOR GOD TO LIE."* Proverbs 14:5: *"A FAITHFUL WITNESS will not lie: But, A FALSE WITNESS will utter lies."* Both God and Calvin are described in that Proverbs passage: One cannot lie; while the other cannot tell the truth! Why? "You are of your father the devil; and the *LUSTS* of your father you will to do. He was a murderer, from the beginning, and abode not in the truth [God's Word], because *THERE IS NO TRUTH IN HIM.* When the devil tells a *LIE,* it is his own [invention]: *Because he is a liar, and THE FATHER of both lies, and liars (John 8:44)." THE DEVIL invented*

Calvin's lies—like he does the lies of other human liars. Romans 1:25 *paints a picture of TREASON against the Creator:* "THEY CHANGED the truth of God *INTO A LIE* [Just as John Calvin did]; *and worshipped and served THE CREATURE MORE THAN THEIR CREATOR.*" Calvin *honored his words over God's Words; so he worshipped himself, a creature, more than God!* Calvin should have taken seriously the warning in James 3:14: "Glory not, and *LIE NOT* against the truth [God's Word]." Because, "*No lie is of the truth* [God's Word] (1 John 2:21)." John Calvin pitted himself against undeniable Bible Truth.

Calvin ALTERING Scripture, to make it SUPPOSEDLY say the OPPOSITE of what was actually written, makes him the liar—Which proves that John Calvin was one of Satan's tools in deceiving God's people. That warns me against trusting any Calvinist doctrine. Calvinism is one of the devil's most deceptive, destructive weapons!

John Calvin's distorted concept of God's Sovereignty BIRTHED all of his other errors. It seems that error was Calvin's only real specialty! John Calvin's view of God's Sovereignty enabled him to explain the existence of evil in the world (*according to a PERVERTED PERCEPTION*): *If God is not behind EVIL as well as GOOD, then God is not Sovereign after all—Calvin concluded. John Calvin's theological system portrays God as desiring creation to experience both good and evil. That ERRONEOUS VIEW of Sovereignty makes Calvinism A MORBID THEOLOGY.* No other theological belief system is any sicker!

Upon that *ERRONEOUS FOUNDATION*, John Calvin *BUILT* a tangled web of deceit, which necessitated that he continue to stack additional lie, upon additional lie, in order to maintain his foundational lies. *This book is exposing those demonic lies with God's Inspired Word!*

71

John Calvin claimed that Divine Sovereignty meant that *GOD PLANNED ADAM'S FALL* (or else, it could not have happened). Then, knowing that all in Adam's race would thereafter be separated from God, and therefore, in a lost, unsaved condition, *God CHOSE to save SOME of Adam's lost offspring—but leave the OTHERS in their lost condition.* And God made those decisions before He created anything. Thus, those decisions were arbitrary on God's part. *A person getting saved or remaining lost was TOTALLY up to God—having nothing to do with the person's own character or personal decisions.* That was God's pre-creation decision—Calvin's *UNCONDITIONAL ELECTION* doctrine. (*The devil's fingerprints all over it!*)

God's chosen ones are designated the ELECT. Those remaining lost are the REPROBATE. And the number of the *ELECT* was also arbitrarily decided before creation. And, of course, the same was true for the *REPROBATE. The REPROBATE cannot possibly be saved, even if they want to be saved*—Which is why Calvin contended that names could neither be blotted out of the Book of Life, nor added to it—no matter what the Bible clearly says. *The devil's fingerprints are definitely on that doctrine!*

John Calvin invented at least three devious tools for his theological *MANEUVERING.* One was his claim that *God ACCOMMODATED Himself to our FEEBLE capacity to understand Bible Truth. Calvin USED that theological ploy wherever the CLEAR Scripture message threatened to expose and destroy his demonic theology.*

In predestination passages that seemed to prove his doctrine, the accommodation trick was unnecessary. He used that ploy chiefly to get himself out of doctrinal tight spots. In Scripture passages, which SEEMED to support Calvinism, God SEEMINGLY spoke plainly. But, in those THAT COULD BE A THREAT TO CALVINISM, God spoke in veiled terms—*which only John Calvin could decipher. But why would God in some passages communicate His true will, while in others have the Bible authors pen the opposite of His ACTUAL intentions? Calvin invented that ACCOMMODATION PLOY. Neither the word nor concept can be found anywhere in Scripture!* (*Hypocrite Calvin!*)

Another favorite theory was Calvin's argument that those whom God said He would blot out were in reality hypocrites—*who SEEMED to be among God's Elect for a time, but were FIGURATIVELY blotted out of the Book of Life.* But, *if those people were hypocrites they were not in the Book of Life! So how could they be blotted out of a Book they were never registered in?* Calvin cut his own theological throat with his own comments. Many think John Calvin was a theological genius—*But his lies and contradictions put him in a different category altogether.* Calvin was a *DECEIVED DECEIVER! And deceivers are not all that smart—for they themselves are deceived!*

John Calvin's third ploy was *his infamous invention he called the SECRET COUNSEL OF GOD. When none of his other tricks worked, he would invariably turn to his claim that we have to accept his interpretation, because it was based on the SECRET WILL of God.* Although not visibly expressed in the Scriptures, there was no other reasonable explanation. Yet, Calvin chided anyone else who appealed to their reasoning for their explanations. *Only he was free to make such interpretative decisions.*

How did John Calvin happen upon such revelation? How did he discover God's *SECRET will? What was his secret in knowing what was SECRET to everyone else?* The fact that Calvin used those maneuvers in so many doctrinal areas reveals that he lacked biblical support in just that many doctrinal areas. *So he just lied a lot!*

It is most suspicious that John Calvin accused the apostle Paul of being deceived when he said in Romans 7:9 that he was at one time alive, then died; *WHEREAS ALL* of Paul's comments regarding predestination were definitely Holy-Spirit inspired. Hmm! John Calvin also maligned the inspired words of Exodus 32:32; claiming that what Moses said unto God there revealed that he was full of pride, his words were confused, and that he spoke as one possessed. Possessed by what? *A demon?* Was that one passage of Exodus inspired by the devil? And the rest by the Holy Spirit? What else could Calvin have meant? *Why did Calvin dispute that one Scripture passage, while offering no resistance to non-threatening passages?* If Calvin were right, then how may we know *WHICH* verses in Moses' writings were *INFLUENCED* by demons, and which were inspired by the *HOLY SPIRIT? Do Calvin's followers ever ask such questions???????*

If the apostle Paul was deceived in what he wrote in one passage in one of his letters, then what confidence could we have that Paul penned the truth in any of his letters? Second Timothy 3:16 tells us that all Scripture is inspired by the Holy Spirit: *ALL—NOT JUST PART!*

All of Calvin's theological errors were the inevitable results of his *unbiblical view of God's Sovereignty; and his STUBBORN determination to hold onto that view no matter what the Scriptures teach. (Calvin the hypocrite!)*

As a God-called New Testament Teacher, I must do whatever I can *TO INFORM* believers and non-believers of the dangers and pitfalls of Calvinism. This volume is no joke. Calvinism is the big *JOKE* the devil has played on the church! And John Calvin was the human joker. *The devil used him to pull that foul joke on the church!*

Chapter IX

Calvinism—a Demonic Conspiracy

While this book exposes Calvinism as a conspiracy, *it is NOT as much the conspiracy of John Calvin as it IS the conspiracy of the devil himself through John Calvin. I do not believe that John Calvin consciously PLANNED to conspire against God and the Protestant church. I am convinced, however, that the devil deceived Calvin, and then used his twisted mindset to deceive MULTITUDES.* Calvinism is the devil's conspiracy against the church. *CALVIN'S DERANGED DOCTRINES have been DRILLED into the Protestant MINDSET over the past five hundred years.* That is half the length of the "Dark Ages" people went through under Medieval Roman Catholicism!

I am sure theologians and other Christians will get offended at me *for saying NEGATIVE things about John Calvin—but even John Calvin's lies are still lies!* He had no special standing with the Almighty. Popularity is no guarantee of Divine approval: "What is highly esteemed among men is abomination to God (Luke 16:15)."

The *DEVIL'S* plan to steal, kill and destroy *coincides with John Calvin's theology precisely.* John Calvin said the devil *ONLY* does what *GOD COMMANDS HIM* to do. That is a demonic *LIE* designed to deceive the religious mind. *NO Scripture passage says any such thing. John Calvin got that LIE from the devil himself!* Naturally, the devil is advantaged if people believe that lie. *And Satan has had that BENEFIT for five centuries! Could the devil persuade John Calvin to convince others that God was behind all the TRAGEDIES he was heaping on mankind, what better*

CAMOUFLAGE for his evil deeds? And John Calvin obliged the devil; and then some. And multitudes patronize John Calvin to this very day. Mind-boggling!

To John Calvin, *Sovereignty meant that nothing can occur in God's universe, other than what God designed; and in His PROVIDENCE MAKES SURE HAPPENS.* That includes *BOTH* good and evil. *The devil is merely a tool in God's hands, carrying out His SECRET WILL*—which, by the way, *CANNOT BE FOUND in any Scripture*—only in Calvin's demonic theology. (*Coincidence?????????*)

It is *NO* coincidence that many cases in which John Calvin resorted to *GOD'S SECRET WILL* had to do with suffering and loss—especially in the believer's life. Is it not obvious that such doctrines fit the devil's agenda? *Rather than the devil being a TOOL in the hand of God, to achieve His secret will, Calvinism was and is a TOOL of the devil, enabling him to steal, kill and destroy, with little or no hindrance!* If suffering truly does glorify God, then what faithful Christian would not accept suffering as something good? But, believers who believe that are thoroughly deceived—Which is why Satan continues to get away with his evil, destructive shenanigans.

John Calvin did not teach that God created the devil AS the devil. He said Lucifer, having been created good, brought that fallen condition upon himself. Yet, Calvin's concept of God's Sovereignty contends that no creature can act on its own. *Nothing happens EXCEPT what God preplanned to happen.* Still, *Lucifer's fall was Lucifer's own fault—Calvin taught.* (*INCONSISTENCY galore!*)

Thus, we have to conclude, either that Lucifer acted independent of God—*which Calvin said cannot happen; or, God FORCED Lucifer to become evil.* From the moral point of view, *what real difference would it make if God created the devil AS the devil, or PLANNED that Lucifer would fall from his original state and become the devil?*

CALVIN WAS PROFICIENT AT CONTRADICTING HIS OWN THEOLOGY WITH HIS OWN THEOLOGY. On one hand, insisting that the devil was the cause of his own fall, while on the other hand, saying nobody can act on his own initiative—*which Calvin was correct? Intelligent believers will question why the Creator, being Sovereign as He is, would opt not only to permit evil to exist in His universe, but EVEN INTEND that evil exist, and become prominent, under His Divine Dominion.*

Calvin insisted that his theology *MUST* be accepted without question; and *that we ought not to pry into the DIVINE SECRETS! HOW DID JOHN CALVIN DISCOVER GOD'S SECRET WILL UNLESS HE PRIED INTO IT? And, why would God not use His Sovereignty to make every creature GOOD? If creation cannot alter the ARBITRARY DESTINY God planned for it, why did He not make ALL creation perfectly good? Calvinism questions God's very character—PORTRAYING HIM AS A MONSTER—proving that Calvinism is the real monster! CALVINISM IS ONE OF SATAN'S MOST DESTRUCTIVE WEAPONS AGAINST THE CHURCH! (Destroying the church FROM WITHIN!)*

When facing a *FORK* in the road ahead, if *ONLY* one path is the *RIGHT* path, if the traveller takes the wrong path and keeps going, the farther he or she travels, *the farther from the right way he or she strays*—The perfect description of John Calvin. *Assuming the only possible perspective of God's Sovereignty was HIS OWN, he built his entire theological system upon that—then lambasted everyone who dared to question his theology—claiming that was the same as questioning the Bible! Oh really?*

77

In Calvin's attempt to protect God's Sovereignty—As though God would need any kind of protection—or could NOT protect Himself—Calvin demeaned the Sovereignty of GOD! Calvin said the ONLY REASON God could know what would occur in the future was His PREPLANNING EVERYTHING that would take place in the future. God's foreknowledge was BASED ON His fore-planning—for it could happen NO OTHER WAY. Thus, *CALVIN LIMITED God's foreknowing ABILITY to His fore-planning action.* Calvin's *TAKE* on Divine Sovereignty did not *TAKE* into account God's unlimited wisdom. His understanding is infinite. In a later chapter, *we will learn what the Bible actually teaches about Divine Sovereignty!*

On the foundation of a distorted view of Sovereignty, Calvin built his next level of theological FALSEHOOD. If nothing can occur except what our Creator preplanned to occur—*then the rise of EVIL in this universe must be connected to God's Sovereignty.* God had to plan evil as well as good! According to Calvin, then, *EVEN Lucifer's fall—and his becoming the devil and Satan—had to be God's will! Then God SENT THE DEVIL to the Garden of Eden to tempt Adam and Eve to SIN.* To make sure His plan worked, God withheld His *GRACE* from Adam and Eve, so they would not be able to resist the temptation. And in Adam's fall, mankind became Totally Depraved.

Although NO Scripture offers even a HINT that such ever occurred, we KNOW (???) that God's SECRET WILL caused that to occur. (Surely you KNOW the devil would want people—especially church people—to believe such Calvinist garbage as this—TOXIC Calvinist garbage!)

Calvin gleaned that lie from *AUGUSTINE'S* writings. Thus, Augustine was a heretic long before John Calvin was. (See the Institutes, book 3, chapter 23, sections 7 and 8.) God had planned in prehistory that man would sin, and need redemption. But, for reasons known only to God Himself, *He decided to redeem only certain ones of Adam's fallen race. God made a secret LIST of people He wanted to SAVE* (by an arbitrary choice)—*the rest of mankind being reprobates*—lost, and offered no hope of salvation. The number on each list was established: *No additions and no deletions. No one could be erased from the Elect list.* And, the Elect list being small in number, *the majority of mankind was BARRED from redemption.* God arbitrarily *DOOMED* them! Since man was Totally Depraved *he was unable to even desire to be saved.* So, individuals who would eventually be *SAVED,* and those who would *REMAIN LOST, WAS DETERMINED BY THE ARBITRARY WILL OF GOD—having nothing to do with a person's character or personal decisions and actions.*

Such was Calvin's Unconditional Election doctrine. *Sinners had no say in either becoming one of the Elect, or REMAINING FOREVER LOST—for God had in eternity past made that DECISION FOR each human being.* That is *PURE* Calvinism! *If you can call the devil's plan pure! And Calvinism is one of the devil's camouflaged plans.*

And if only a CERTAIN NUMBER of the lost had been elected to salvation, then Christ needed not to shed His blood FOR ANY BUT HIS ELECT. So, the next deception was the Limited Atonement doctrine. John Calvin went to great lengths to convince himself and others of that falsehood—*but was not able to prove it—so he appealed to GOD'S SUPPOSED SECRET WILL. Finding NO biblical proof of that doctrine, he invented his own proof.* And to this day, countless church members are strung out on Calvin's demonic falsehoods! *Calvinism is nothing more than A RELIGIOUS DRUG—STUPEFYING MULTITUDES by some of the most deceptive demonic lies in existence.*

The next heretical doctrine, built upon the previous falsehood of Limited Atonement, was Irresistible Grace. God's will being immutable, and He having preplanned to save a *CERTAIN NUMBER* of people, *He had put into place a system which ASSURED that the Elect would be brought safely into the fold. If one was on that Elect list, then he or she would be saved no matter what. Nobody could RESIST the secret work of the Holy Spirit in his or her soul.* That cannot be found anywhere in the Bible!

The final deceptive doctrine of five-point-Calvinism is the Perseverance of the Saints—Once-Saved-Always-Saved. *Each consecutive unbiblical doctrine sprang from the previous ungodly falsehood of Calvin's TULIP.*

Once-Saved-always-Saved is a demonic *LIE*—rather than a biblical promise. All five points of Calvinism are either true or false. *They ALL rise or fall together.* Thus, *the VALIDITY of each point depends on the genuineness of ALL the others. Proving that just one of the five points is INVALID automatically renders ALL the rest INVALID: The ENTIRE Calvinist system collapses! And MULTIPLE Scriptures prove that EACH of the five TULIP TENETS is false.* But, it is necessary to address only a few here.

Whereas Calvin taught that Jesus shed His blood for only a small portion of the lost—Limited Atonement—*a number of Scriptures prove without doubt that our Lord sacrificed Himself upon the cross for the ENTIRE human race.* Luke 19:10 is one: *Jesus stated there that He had come to save WHAT WAS LOST.* His words contain *NOT* even a hint that He referred only to a small percentage of the lost. He obviously meant *ALL* the lost—Scripture number one. Romans 5:6 also says Christ died for the ungodly—*Not a mere portion of the ungodly, but ALL the ungodly!* Surely, *all will agree that all of fallen mankind is ungodly!* So, if Christ died for the ungodly—Romans 5:6—*but ONLY for the Elect—Calvin's idea*—then *ONLY THE ELECT MUST BE UNGODLY.* All others are saints. However, *ALL human beings BEING ungodly by nature, then Christ died for ALL human beings. The ONLY REAL saints are those who are IN Christ—None outside Him!*

Now, according to the Bible, ALL doctrines have to be established by two, or more, witnesses. We have looked at *TWO* witnesses. Third witness—Romans 11:32—God confined *ALL* under disobedience, that He might *HAVE MERCY ON ALL. God offers salvation to the VERY SAME ALL He confined under disobedience!* Calvin denied the clear wording of that passage, in order to maintain his false doctrine. *Calvin literally REWROTE Romans 11:32 by claiming Paul only meant that those who are saved* —meaning the Elect—*ought to ascribe their salvation to God's mercy; for God did not provide salvation for every sinner.* Thus, *CALVINISM IS A DOCTRINE OF DEMONS,* according to 1 Timothy 4:1. Check that out.

Need more proof? In 1 Timothy 1:15, Paul said that Jesus came to earth to save sinners. *All outside Christ being sinners, then it is evident that Christ came to save all human beings!* We *ALSO* read in 1 Timothy 2:4 that *GOD WANTS ALL MEN TO BE SAVED.* Calvin attempted to offset that Bible Truth by contending that Paul only meant that *God wants some from every ethnic group to be saved. He did not mean every human being in every ethnic group. But God DOES WANT ALL to be saved,* so Calvin's Limited Atonement doctrine *GOES DOWN THE TUBE! And all the other TULIP TENETS go down with it.*

First Timothy 2:6 tells us that Jesus gave Himself a ransom for *ALL*; thus providing salvation for *ALL. John Calvin said Paul only meant ALL of the Special Elect, for Christ did not become a ransom for every human being on earth.* (????) Scripture proves John Calvin's Limited Atonement doctrine to be a falsehood—spawned by the devil himself. *Calvinism is pro-lie and anti-truth!*

In 2 Peter 3:9, God's will appeared in reverse terms: Peter saying God is not willing that any should perish: Another way of saying that God wants *ALL* to be saved. Calvin contended that Peter was only talking about the Elect—*God does not want any of the Elect to perish.* He *DOES WANT* the Reprobate to *PERISH* in Hades for His glory. *Calvinism is a hateful, sick, demonic theology!*

Hebrews 2:9 *tells us plainly that Jesus tasted death for EVERY human being.* Again, Calvin said that merely meant *every Elect human being—not everyone on earth.* Christ's sacrifice bypassed the Reprobate. (?????????)

In CERTAIN Scripture passages containing the word world, Calvin said those writers had in mind only God's Elect—not every human being on earth. For instance: In John 1:29, John the Baptizer said Jesus was the Lamb of God, *Who takes away the sin of the WHOLE WORLD.* Calvin claimed that the word *WORLD* there means only *THE ELECT.* In 1 John 1:2, John said that Jesus is the propitiation for our sins—*and not only for our sins, but also for the sins of the WHOLE world. Calvin contended that WORLD in that verse meant ONLY THE ELECT who were scattered abroad—not all sinners inhabiting earth.*

In those passages that contained the word world but posed no threat to Calvin's theology, world JUST meant world. John Calvin never let the Bible stand in the way of what HE WANTED TO BELIEVE. If he did not like the way a passage was worded, he would REWORD it until it agreed with his theology. (Demonic manipulation!) Satan manipulated Calvin to manipulate the church.

Calvin even went *SO FAR* as to insinuate that what came out of God's own mouth was false. Exodus 32:33 is a prime example. God said that He would blot out of His book anybody who sinned against Him. Calvin said that could not happen. Thus, *in order to STUBBORNLY HOLD ONTO his demonic theology, Calvin implied that the Sovereign Creator Himself is a LIAR.* The devil being the father of lies, then the devil has to be the father of Calvinism! Moses penned Exodus 32:32-33, and John Calvin *SAID* Moses lied. In Psalms 69:28, David spoke of blotting names out of God's Book of Life, and Calvin *CLAIMED* that David lied. Ezekiel 13:9 *establishes that names ARE NOT SET IN CONCRETE in the Book of Life.* Names can be subtracted from or added to the Book of Life. Calvin rebuked Ezekiel too! Revelation 3:5 records Jesus' words to the effect that the names of those who overcome will never be blotted out of the Book of Life— *indicating that names of those who fail to overcome will be blotted out. So Calvin would have to rebuke Jesus as well for telling an untruth* (according to John Calvin). In Revelation 22:19, Jesus said that if anyone takes away from the words of the prophecies of that book, God will take away his part out of the Book of Life! Thus, Calvin would rebuke the Father, His Son, the Holy Spirit, and the apostle John *FOR LYING* in the Book of Revelation. How can anybody honestly believe John Calvin's words over the inspired words of the Father, Son, Holy Spirit, Moses, David, Ezekiel and the apostles Paul and John? *Siding with John Calvin is siding with the devil himself. Taking sides against God, His Word, and His church!*

The devil needed someone gullible, and found him in John Calvin. Calvin's personal gullibility, and his ability to talk other people into believing that HIS theology was the correct one, turned out to be a POWERFUL ASSET to Satan in his attacks against God and His church.

Further complicating those matters, the longevity of Calvinism (about five hundred years) makes Calvinism *SEEM* to have *GOD'S STAMP OF APPROVAL*. However, *longevity does not turn demonic lies into Bible Truth!*

Wrapping up this chapter, I want to ask a couple of *thought-provoking questions*. One: *"If Calvinism truly is the one and only correct theology—that EVERY thought, word, and action OF EVERY HUMAN BEING HAPPENS BECAUSE GOD HAS WILLED THEM TO HAPPEN, then WHY did John Calvin think it necessary to fight Roman Catholicism, Arminianism, or ANY other theology? John Calvin's own actions suggested that the actions of those other theologians were not of God—whereas Calvin said that nobody could take any action which was not God's will. According to Calvin's OWN theology, those fighting his theology had to be in God's will.* Calvinism is *MOST INCONSISTENT! (And undeniably ultra-stupid!)*

Question number two—If it is *TRUE* that everything that happens happens the way it happens *BECAUSE* it is God's will to happen that way, then why pray? *What good does it do to pray for certain results that we want, if the results GOD WANTS in our lives are the results we will get? That is not a HYPOTHETICAL CONCERN! Most preachers today teach that religious lie. It is rampant in most Bible commentaries—and almost every prayer and sermon. And they got that unreasonable reasoning from John Calvin's unreasonable demonic theology!*

Calvinism is just a pathetic attempt to replace God's Word with HUMAN reason—which cannot match God's wisdom or power. Life is in God's Living Word. Death is in Calvinism. Those who attack God's Word are setting themselves up for destruction in both this life and the next. *Flee Calvinism and all other demonic theologies!*

Chapter X

The real Divine Predestination

The primary purpose of this book is *NOT to demean Bible Truth about Predestination and God's Sovereignty; but rather to expose John Calvin's deceptive distortions of those biblical doctrines; then present the biblical truth regarding them.* I will need to *REPEAT* some of Calvin's theological errors which we have previously discussed, in order to *CONTRAST* them with what Scripture really says about *SOVEREIGNTY* and *PREDESTINATION*. This chapter focuses on *DIVINE PREDESTINATION, and* the following chapter on *DIVINE SOVEREIGNTY.*

Bible Truth about PREDESTINATION: First of all, the Greek word translated predestination occurs *ONLY* six times in the entire New Testament (Acts 4:28, Romans 8:29-30, 1 Corinthians 2:7 and Ephesians 1:5 and 11). At times, used in connection with predestination is the word *FOREKNOW* or *FOREKNOWLEDGE;* which occurs as well only a *FEW* times in the entire New Testament. Nevertheless, *John Calvin made predestination the very centerpiece of his theology*—all based upon a *BIZARRE, UNBIBLICAL CONCEPT* of God's Sovereignty.

Before proceeding, I will share with you a truth that the preacher E. W. Kenyon learned from the Lord long ago—one which has aided him and other truth-seekers (including myself) in *RIGHTLY dividing the Word of God* (2 Timothy 2:15). The preacher, E. W. Kenyon, became concerned about how to *AVOID* misunderstanding and misrepresenting God's Word, so he asked the Lord how he could know for certain *IF* a doctrine was either valid or invalid for Christians to believe. Then, the Lord told him: "If the underlying concept is found in the Book of Genesis in seed form, then in the Law of Moses as type or shadow (form of *PROPHECY*), then in the Psalms, as prophecy in song, then in the Old Testament prophets, as biblical prophecy, then in the Gospels, as taught by Christ, then in the Book of Acts, as experienced by the church, then in the New Testament Letters, as written doctrine, such doctrine is Heaven-approved." *The exact wording of the doctrine does not have to appear in any of the seven Scripture sections*—just the concept. If the substance of any doctrine cannot be found in all seven sections, then that doctrine is at least questionable.

So, let us look into the doctrine of predestination to find out whether John Calvin's understanding of it was biblical. First we will search those *SEVEN* areas of Holy Scripture for the underlying concept of predestination; starting in Genesis, the seed-form book. The term seed form means that only limited information can be found in Genesis; *for a seed is only the beginning. In later Old Testament books revelation grows. What begins in seed form is gradually developed until it becomes fully ripe in the New Testament.* (Genesis-to-Revelation-revelation)

The fact that God created the universe PROVES that He had some definite purpose in mind for every created entity. Otherwise, why would the Creator have brought anything into being? *Thus, God did create everything to experience some PREPLANNED DESTINY. So in the very first book of the Bible, we do see predestination in seed form.* Creation was created for a Divine Purpose!

But, not every created being accepted God's original purpose for their existence. Jude six says that early on *SOME* of the angels rebelled against both their position and function, which God had designed for them. Isaiah 14:12-15 and Ezekiel 28:11-19 *are records of the tragic story of Lucifer, ONE of the chief angels, who incited an ancient celestial rebellion against his own Creator.* Also see 1 Timothy 3:6, and Revelation 12:3-4, 7-9. Genesis 3:1-6 *tells about that fallen angel showing up on earth and contaminating God's later creation—mankind.*

Genesis 3:15 *reveals that first SEED of the Creator's predetermined plan to REDEEM the human race.* Jesus Christ proved to be the Seed of the woman, Who would crush Satan's head—Authority. Thus, *Genesis reveals the FIRST prophecy of the coming of the Redeemer—*and that in *SEED FORM.* But He was not only the Woman's Seed prophesied in Genesis 3:15, but *ALSO* the Seed of Abraham (Galatians 3:16)—Whom God sent to redeem the human race by destroying the devil's *ILLEGAL* hold on humanity. First section—seed-form doctrine.

Now to the Law, the second Scripture section which must contain a doctrine as type or shadow; if it is to be considered a valid Christian doctrine. Predestination of Christ surfaces again in Numbers 21:9 in the *FORM* of *TYPE.* In response to Moses' prayer for the people, God instructed Moses to fasten a bronze serpent on a pole, and have the people gaze upon it, in order to be healed from snakebite. That was a type of Christ on the cross, as proven by our Savior's own words in John 3:14: *"As Moses lifted up the serpent on a pole, so the Son of Man must be lifted up* [on a cross]." *Predestination of Christ!*

Types and shadows of the coming Redeemer appear in *MORE* than one of Moses' Law Books. But, it will be necessary to provide only a *FEW* examples to establish the *FACT* that *PREDESTINATION* of Jesus Christ as the Messiah is a God-approved biblical doctrine.

Exodus 17:6 foreshadows Christ; explained by Paul in 1 Corinthians 10:4. Leviticus chapter sixteen (*about two goats on the Day of Atonement*) also typifies Christ.

In Psalms 16, 22 and 110, we find *prophecies of the preplanned sufferings of the Messiah in His redemption of mankind.* If one of those prophecies is proven to be part of God's predestination plan, then all of them are, because all of them are interconnected. Thus, *Christ's predestination appears in the Psalms in song-prophecy:* Section number three. Then, Scripture-Section four,...

The Old Testament prophets: The most well-known prophecy regarding the sufferings of the Messiah is in Isaiah chapter fifty-three. Isaiah prophesied God would place on His Messiah every human sin—along with all due punishment—*including sickness and other human ailments.* Zechariah 13:6-7 foretold the suffering of our Redeemer, as did some other Old Testament prophets. Jeremiah and Ezekiel prophesied the *NEW BIRTH*—the result of the Savior's predetermined sacrifice (Jeremiah 31:31-34; Ezekiel 36:26). Then the next section,...

In the Gospels, the *LORD* Himself prophesied of His *PREDETERMINED CRUCIFIXION AND RESURRECTION.* Matthew 16:21: "*The Lord showed His disciples that He must go to Jerusalem, and* [there to] *suffer many things from the elders, and chief priests, and scribes—then be killed, and be raised the third day.*" Matthew 17:22-23: "*The Son of Man is about to be betrayed into the hands of men, and they will kill Him, and the third day He will be raised.*" Christ's sacrifice was no accident. In John 10:17-18, Jesus stated: "My Father loves Me because I [voluntarily] lay down My life, that I may take it again. Nobody [*human or demon*] takes it from Me, but I lay it down My own self [*according to God's redemption plan*].

88

I have *POWER* to lay My life down, and I have power to take it again. That command have I received from My Father." *The FACT that God had commanded our Savior to lay down His life PROVES that His sacrifice had been preplanned.* The Almighty had *PURPOSED IT.* Thus, we find the predestination of the Messiah and salvation of mankind in the Gospels—the fifth section of the seven-sectioned principle which determines whether or not a doctrine is valid for us believers to believe. The Gospels prophesy and fulfill prophecies of Christ's sacrifice.

Acts 2:23 agrees, just as had been prophesied, that Jesus Christ was *"delivered up [unto crucifixion] by the determined PURPOSE and foreknowledge of God."* Acts 4:27-28 tells us: "Against Jesus, Herod, Pontius Pilate, the Gentiles and the people of Israel were *ALL* gathered together *to do whatever God had previously determined to be done."* Also see Luke 24:44, Acts 3:24-26, 4:9-12, 13:26-41 and 28:23 for further testimony—Section six of that seven-sectioned principle of doctrine-validation. Furthermore, throughout Acts, the church experienced the blessings Jesus Christ purchased on the cross.

The seventh proof is in the letters of Peter and Paul *as actual WRITTEN doctrine.* The best-known Scripture passage concerning predestination—*AND* the Scripture most used by John Calvin to *SUPPOSEDLY* support his theology—is Romans 8:29: *"Whom God FOREKNEW He also PREDESTINED to be conformed to the image of His Son, so that He might be THE FIRSTBORN among many brethren."* Calvin missed the whole point of Paul here.

Ephesians 1:4-5 says: *"God chose us IN HIM* [Jesus Christ] *BEFORE the foundation of the world, so that we should be holy and without blame before* [God] *in love: GOD HAVING PREDESTINED US unto adoption AS sons*

BY Jesus Christ UNTO HIMSELF, according to the good pleasure of God's will." Paul stressed *THE REASON* for predestination rather than *WHO* was predestined. *That reveals Calvin's MISTAKE—emphasizing the word US in those passages. US* was not the goal of predestination. *The goal was predestining us to be CONFORMED to the image of Christ—the very IMAGE of God! Restoring lost human beings BACK TO THE IMAGE AND LIKENESS of God was the PURPOSE of predestination; not arbitrarily predestining a small number of people to be saved!*

Ephesians 1:10: "So that, in the dispensation of the fullness of the times, *He might gather together into one all things in Christ*—both things that are in heaven and things that are on earth; even in Him." Truth is, it was our inheritance that was predestined, not individuals!

Through believing the Gospel, people BECOME THE "ELECT—according to THE FOREKNOWLEDGE OF GOD (1 Peter 1:2)." And, *foreknowledge is not foreordination; although Calvin contended that it was. The real Gospel message is that God foreordained Jesus Christ to make salvation AVAILABLE to ALL who believe God for it. And CONTRARY TO Calvinism, GOD DID NOT DECIDE WHO would believe the Gospel and WHO would not believe it. That choice is the prerogative of every human being!*

"[Jesus Christ,] indeed, was foreordained before the foundation of the world, but was manifest in these last times for you (1 Peter 1:20)." Thus, *predestination and foreordination was all about what Christ accomplished, not about WHO would accept His accomplishments!*

We discovered abundant evidence in seven sections of the Bible that God foreordained Christ to redeem us from sin *AND* its consequences. Bible Predestination *IS*

VALID Christian doctrine! Bible Predestination *IS NOT* Calvinism. And Calvinism *IS NOT* Bible Predestination. Scripture neither teaches, nor supports, Calvinism! No being was ever arbitrarily *CHOSEN* by God to be either saved or lost. Calvin's distorted concept of Sovereignty brought that error into the Protestant church.

In Romans 8:29, *predestination is ABOUT believers being conformed to the image of Christ; not about which individual human beings were supposedly predestined to be saved, and which were arbitrarily rejected—based on God's SECRET WILL.* And, Ephesians 1:5 *focuses on believers coming into sonship* (adoption) *through Jesus Christ*, rather than emphasizing who are the Elect, and who the Reprobate. *Calvinism is contemptible!*

REAL BIBLE PREDESTINATION is all about our Lord bringing into existence certain BENEFITS to be conferred upon people who believe. People who believe the Gospel get the goodies. People who reject the Gospel forfeit the goodies. *GOSPEL-REJECTORS BECOME REPROBATES.* Predestination is about *OUR INHERITANCE IN CHRIST, NOT ABOUT WHO IS FORCED INTO CHRIST, AND WHO IS ARBITRARILY BARRED FROM HIM!*

John Calvin's predestination *THEORY* is a bunch of demonic hogwash. *We found Bible Predestination about Christ (which is what Bible Predestination is ALL about) in all seven Bible sections. You will find Calvin's version of predestination in NO section of the Bible.*

Numerous events in both angelic and human history were not predestined by God. Those events came about through the rebellious wills of some of God's creatures; not God's will, secret or otherwise. Nevertheless, God is in *ULTIMATE CONTROL* of creation! *Nothing will escape*

His scrutiny and judgment! Our Creator gave both men and angels a free will; and will hold every creature fully accountable for the right or wrong use of their free will. *The GUILTY are predestined to ETERNAL PUNISHMENT;* the *FAITHFUL* to *ETERNAL LIFE—Bible Predestination!*

Calvin ignorantly contended that: "*We know that all of those who are adopted to the hope of salvation were written* [in the Book of Life] *before the foundation of the world* (Ephesians 1:4)." "*WE KNOW* on the testimony of Christ, that names of the children of God were written in the Book of Life *FROM* the beginning (Luke 10:20)." See if you can find in Luke 10:20 the words: "the Book of Life from the beginning." *Those words are NOT there!*

Where does Ephesians 1:4 talk about God *WRITING* names in the Book of Life? And what part of Ephesians 1:4 mentions salvation for some being a decision *GOD* made for them? *Calvin could SEE things NOT written in Scripture—blinding himself to what WAS written.*

Calvin emphasized the fact that Ephesians 1:4 says God has chosen *US.* Paul stressed the vehicle by which *US* were chosen—God has chosen us *IN HIM—CHRIST.* That means Paul did not imply that certain people (*US*) were predestined to accept Christ—*but that those who accept Christ are the Elect! Bible Predestination has to do with the Christian's POSITION IN Christ, rather than with WHICH individuals were arbitrarily chosen to be in Christ—"Having predestinated us UNTO the adoption of children by Jesus Christ unto Himself (Ephesians 1:5)." That is what Bible Predestination is all about—*Not God arbitrarily choosing some to be saved and others to be lost. *God wants all to be saved, and provided salvation through Jesus Christ for all to be saved!*

Chapter XI

The real Divine Sovereignty

There is a world of difference between John Calvin's view of God's Sovereignty and Bible Truth about Divine Sovereignty. *To Calvin, Sovereignty meant that God had TO BE IN DIRECT CONTROL of everything that happens in heaven and on earth. EVIL being prevalent on earth, then both good and evil must be God's will!* Otherwise, *God would not be Sovereign after all—for certain events would be beyond His Divine Control.* According to John Calvin, *the very term Sovereignty had to mean that God cannot be limited by any existing power—*including His own. *Limitation of any kind would bring His Sovereignty into question.* Therefore, *Calvin actually limited God by claiming that He could not limit Himself!*

Truth is, God's self-limitation is taught in the Bible. *The inability to LIMIT Himself would certainly bring His Sovereignty into question.* God's very Word teaches that *God CANNOT lie* (Titus 1:2; Hebrews 6:18). That is one Divine limitation. *Neither can God FAIL* (Psalms 89:33; Zephaniah 3:5). *Nor can God COMMIT unrighteousness* (Psalms 92:15; Romans 9:14). *God HAS limited Himself in certain aspects of His CHARACTER and ACTIVITIES. SELF-LIMITATION IS A NECESSARY ATTRIBUTE* of the Sovereign God. John Calvin denied that Bible Reality!

It is quite obvious that God exercised self-limitation when He created man: *If giving man dominion over ALL the rest of creation was not a limitation of Himself, then God's words in* Genesis 1:26-28 *were meaningless.* Of course, John Calvin's theology did make those Genesis words *APPEAR* meaningless. *Calvin insisted that people can neither think, say or do anything OTHER than what GOD HAS DECIDED that they think, say or do—decided BEFORE He created anything!* Where is that said in the Bible? *That must be one of those secret doctrines Calvin could detect between Scripture lines. If the preacher has to build his theology on secret* (that is unrevealed—not actually written in Scripture) *doctrines, then God DOES NOT BACK that man's theology! If the preacher does not get his ministry materials from the Bible, and his power from the Holy Spirit, then from where would he possibly get his revelation? And what gospel would he preach?*

Calvin taught that God's every action is *RIGHT* just because He is *SOVEREIGN. His Sovereignty makes Him right!* Thus, Calvin emphasized God's power. The Bible emphasizes God's righteousness and fairness in all His dealings with creation. *FROM* His righteousness comes His power. The Bible teaches that God is not righteous because He is Sovereign, *BUT* Sovereign because He is righteous! God does what is right for both Himself and all of creation. Every creature is treated properly.

One Scripture Calvin *USED* to promote his theology was Isaiah 46:10—in which God said He: "Declared the end from the beginning, and from ancient times, those things which are not yet done, saying: 'My counsel will stand, and *I WILL* do all My pleasure.'" To John Calvin, that meant that God had planned all things that would happen—good and evil. *He interpreted that passage as saying the REASON God could declare the end from the beginning was that He predestined in the beginning all things that would happen throughout history. So Calvin EMPHASIZED GOD'S OMNIPOTENCE AT THE EXPENSE OF HIS WISDOM.* But, God's Sovereignty is manifested through His unlimited Wisdom. The Creator is so *WISE* and *POWERFUL,* that He is *ABLE* to cause His ultimate plans to *PREVAIL* in the final wrap-up—*even if many of His creatures ATTEMPT to thwart His ultimate plans by THEIR rebellion.* Furthermore, Isaiah 46:10 *DOES NOT SAY that everything that happens is God's WILL.* It just says that what He has planned will eventually win out. When God's ultimate plan is finally realized, His mercy and justice will have *PREVAILED.* In no way did Isaiah teach that the Creator is the *CAUSE OF EVERY EVENT IN HISTORY!* That is more demonic Calvinist garbage.

NO Scripture suggests that God planned that there be a devil, or sin, or Lake of Fire! Matthew 25:41 *DOES NOT SAY* that the Lake of Fire was *CREATED*—but that it was *PREPARED.* The Greek word translated prepared is not the word for created. John Calvin, being a Greek scholar, *SHOULD HAVE KNOWN THAT.* So, *Calvin was either NOT ALL THAT SMART, or he was DISHONEST in his dealing with that Scripture passage. PREPARATION IS NOT CREATION. Preparation JUDGES what has been created already. THAT LAKE OF FIRE WAS PREPARED AFTER LUCIFER AND ONE THIRD OF GOD'S ANGELS REBELLED.* Notice that *Matthew DID NOT SAY that the Lake of Fire was prepared FOR LUCIFER AND OTHER RANDOMLY CHOSEN unlucky angels, but for the DEVIL and those other angelic REBELS. HELL DID NOT EXIST BEFORE LUCIFER FELL and became God's archenemy.* There was no need for Hell before that *FIRST* rebellion.

Reference to the angel-rebel called Lucifer in Isaiah 14:12-15, more about him is revealed in Ezekiel 28:15: "*You were perfect in all of your ways from the day that you were created, until iniquity was found in you.*" *Only then was Hell PREPARED to punish the angelic rebels!* God *DID NOT PLAN* for evil to exist in this universe; yet *EVIL DOES PREVAIL ON EARTH.* And because evil does exist,

John Calvin taught that God *MUST* have planned that evil be part of His overall purpose for His creation. *NOT SO! EVIL was the devil's PLAN for the earth and all of God's creation.* Calvin's theology *BLASPHEMES* God!

Scripture clearly reveals that the Creator gave to all intelligent creatures a *FREE WILL*—so that each might *SERVE HIM VOLUNTARILY.* John 4:23 says God seeks those who will worship Him in spirit and in truth: That means worshipping God because one desires to do so.

By giving all intelligent creatures a *FREE WILL,* God *RISKED* the possibility that some might not voluntarily worship or obey Him. But *DUE TO His Infinite Wisdom, God was not caught unprepared when SOME creatures did use their free will to REBEL against Him. Foreseeing rebellion would occur, He was READY for it when it did occur.* But, God also foresaw many doing what He had hoped they would—Worship and obey Him voluntarily, out of love and true appreciation. *Many have PLEASED their Creator throughout human history—and will do so throughout eternity.* Thus, God's *WISE AND GRACIOUS* dealings with His creation are vindicated both now and forever. God is smarter than Calvin credited Him to be.

God has no plan *B*—only plan *A*. Calvin also taught that God only had plan *A*—but, *claimed evil was part of His plan A.* Truth is, *God's plan A does not include evil, but keeps evil IN CHECK through His Sovereignty; while He brings plan A to full fruition for both Himself and His faithful creatures. God knows how His creation works!*

When Isaiah wrote in Isaiah 46:10, "My counsel will stand, and *I will do all My pleasure,*" John Calvin took that to mean that every event in all angelic and human history, both good and evil, was pleasing to God. *Why?*

God had obviously PLANNED that those things happen! (Calvin's interpretation) However, *that passage actually proves the very opposite to be true.* For God did not say that all angelic and human activities pleased Him, but rather that He would do all *HIS* pleasure (despite what men and angels do)! In other words, *God will have HIS WAY in the end, no matter how any of His creatures act on their own.* God only said that His counsel will stand *IN THE FACE OF ANY AND ALL REBELLION.* In mercy, God delivers and blesses *ALL* those who cooperate with Him; *BUT, REPAYS ALL REBELS TO THEIR VERY FACE* (Deuteronomy 7:10; Romans 12:19). *NO Scripture even hints that God predestined certain humans and angels to become rebels.* In *EVERY* Bible case, men and angels made such decisions on their own. God forces no being to be either obedient, or disobedient! *John Calvin lied!*

In Deuteronomy 30:19, God said: "I call heaven and earth to record this day against you—that *I HAVE SET BEFORE YOU LIFE AND DEATH; BOTH BLESSING AND CURSING*: Therefore, choose life [*AND* blessing], so that both you and all your seed [offspring] may live [*AND* be blessed]." *God commanded those people to do their own choosing!* His part was setting before them the choices.

Iniquity *WAS FOUND IN* Lucifer *AFTER* his creation; not *FORCED UPON* him either at, or after, his creation! (Ezekiel 28:15) *IF GOD HAD PUT SIN IN LUCIFER, WHY DID EZEKIEL SAY THAT SIN WAS FOUND IN HIM?*

To get this Bible message across, I will ask a couple of questions. One: Is sin a created thing? Two: Did God create sin? According to Scripture, sin is not a created thing, but rather, the perversion of created things. God created sex (male and female to be joined in marriage); but adultery and homosexuality are perversions of sex.

97

Sin therefore is a perversion of creation, not something that God created. *Our Creator did not create murder, or adultery, or theft, or homosexuality, or lying.* John 8:44 *tells us the devil invented the lie.* So sin is not the work of our Creator. *Created beings using THEIR FREE WILL to pervert themselves and others is the source of sin.*

God is personally responsible for neither the concept nor commission of sin. Sin BEGAN with Lucifer, the first rebel—who then spread his rebellion and perversion far and wide—especially on earth (Romans 1:18-32, 5:12).

The FACT that many of God's creatures are rebelling in no way suggests that He is not Sovereign—or that He is not in ULTIMATE CONTROL of creation. In the Book of Revelation *we see God as the Righteous Judge METING out justice to both the righteous and the wicked.*

The righteous will receive their REWARDS at the first resurrection. A thousand years later, *at the Great White Throne Judgment, record books which heaven has kept from the beginning will reveal everything that EVIL men and angels have committed during their existence. Then the wicked will be judged from those record books. That Tribunal is not for the righteous, but for the WICKED.* Its purpose is not to determine if one is saved, or lost, but the *DEGREE* of punishment the sinner standing before God will be subjected to in the Lake of Fire for eternity. *The Bible clearly teaches that there will be DEGREES of punishment in the Lake of Fire, as there will be LEVELS of reward for those who have lived righteously on earth.* (The rewards will be received at the first resurrection.)

Rebellion that demands severe punishment primarily deals with people's NEGATIVE RESPONSE to the Gospel message. Matthew 10:14-15 says: *"Whosoever does not receive you* [as My God-ordained messengers], *or hear* [meaning to believe and accept] *your* [Gospel] *words, it will be MORE tolerable for Sodom and Gomorrah on the day of judgment THAN IT WILL BE for that* [rebellious] *city."* *MORE tolerable for some means LESS tolerable for others.* That speaks of punishment in the Lake of Fire; which will be *PERMANENT PUNISHMENT—forever!*

Matthew 11:20-24: *"Then began He to upbraid those cities wherein most of His mighty works had been done;* because they repented not: 'Woe to you, Chorazin! Woe to you, Bethsaida! For if those mighty works that have been done in you had been done in [ancient] Tyre and Sidon, *they would have REPENTED a long time ago in sackcloth and ashes.* Therefore, I tell you that it will be *MORE* tolerable for Tyre and Sidon *ON* Judgment Day, than it will be for you [who have heard God's Word but did not repent]. And you, Capernaum, who are exalted to heaven, will be brought down to Hell: Because, if the mighty works which have been *DONE IN YOU* had been *DONE IN SODOM*, it would have remained to *THIS* very day. But I say to you, that it will be *MORE* tolerable for the land of Sodom on the Day of Judgment than it will for you.'" Luke 12:47-48: "That servant, who knew His Lord's will, but prepared not himself, nor did according to His will, will be beaten *WITH MANY STRIPES* [receive greater punishment]. *But he who knew not* [the Lord's will], *but committed things which are worthy of stripes* [punishment], *WILL BE BEATEN* with few[er stripes]."

Believers too will receive varying degrees of reward. "We [Christians] must all appear before the Judgment Seat of Christ—that each [of us] may receive the things done in our body, according to *ALL* that we have done; whether it be good or bad [gaining reward, or suffering loss] (2 Corinthians 5:10)." Further explanation,...

"No other foundation can anyone lay than what has been laid—the Lord Jesus Christ. If one builds on that foundation with gold, silver, precious stones—or wood, hay, or straw—each believer's work will be exposed; for the day [of Christian judgment] will reveal whether the work is good or evil by *FIRE*. For that fire will test each one's work, of what sort it is. If anybody's work that he has built upon that foundation endures, he will receive a reward. But if anybody's work is burned, then he will suffer loss; *yet the believer him or herself will be saved*; yet so as through fire (1 Corinthians 3:11-15)."

"I [Paul] have fought the good fight [of faith]; I have finished my [*Christian and ministry*] course; and I have kept the Bible Faith: Henceforth there is laid up for me the crown of righteousness, which our Lord Jesus, the Righteous Judge, will give me *ON THAT DAY. BUT NOT TO ME ONLY*, but also to everyone who loves the Lord's appearing [who are looking for Him] (2 Timothy 4:7-8)."

Romans 2:16: "[On some future] day God will judge *THE SECRETS OF MEN* by Jesus Christ—according to my Gospel." That judgment concerns *MEN'S SECRETS*, not God's *SUPPOSED SECRET WILL! Calvin was either totally IGNORANT of God's Bible Will—or he deliberately lied about God's will in his written works!* Now this:

We CHRISTIANS will be judged only for any sins we have purposely committed as Christians; and have not repented of, or confessed—Because all of our past sins were washed away by Christ's *BLOOD* (Revelation 1:5). *ALL* of the old sinful things of our past life have passed away (2 Corinthians 5:17). *Believers will not be judged for any sins they committed before being born again!*

Chapter XII

God's Word versus Calvinism

Contrary to John Calvin's claims, there is no *BIBLE EVIDENCE* that God made an Elect list before creation. He certainly *DID NOT* decide to withhold salvation from the majority of the human race for some *MYSTERIOUS PURPOSE*—which Scripture does not reveal, but which Calvin had inside information on. (?????) *Calvin's Total Depravity doctrine is an OUTRIGHT Demonic deception. Which means Unconditional Election is a FRAUDULENT doctrine. That renders Limited Atonement a lie as well. And that, in turn, leaves no place for Irresistible Grace.* God does not force anyone into His Kingdom. Nor does He *SHUT THE DOOR* in the face of any who want to get into His Kingdom. *Biblical salvation is a whosoever-will proposition.* Judgment is for whosoever *WILL NOT!* And the Bible Reality that names *MAY BE* blotted out of the Book of Life *proves that Once-Saved-Always-Saved is a subtle demonic lie too.* So, Perseverance of the Saints is also an *INVALID* doctrine. *NO BIBLE FOR IT!*

The insinuation that some of the Bible writers were mistaken in some of the things they wrote, or that God had them write in accommodation to *our LOW capacity to grasp Calvinist truth, shows how DESPERATE Calvin was to maintain his false doctrines*—And how powerful Satan was in blinding John Calvin—and then through him blinding multitudes for five whole centuries.

To the Jews, Jesus said that although He had come in His Father's name, they would not believe Him. But, *if some other man came IN HIS OWN NAME, they would*

101

believe him (John 5:43). *Paul said essentially the same to Christians in Corinth* (2 Corinthians 11:4). Jeremiah 5:31: "The prophets prophesy falsely, and those priests rule their own way—*and My people LOVE to have it so.*" Isaiah 30:10: *The people begged their prophets: "Do not prophesy to us right things—speak to us smooth things: Prophesy deceits."* Many *JEWS* in olden days *WANTED TO BE DECEIVED. And many in the MODERN CHURCH ALSO WANT TO BE DECEIVED! CALVINISM ATTRACTS THAT KIND OF PEOPLE!* Woe to deception-desirers!

There is plenty of Bible *SUPPORT* for *CONDITIONAL SALVATION—Which is available to ALL who WILLINGLY receive it. ETERNAL SECURITY is promised ONLY to the FAITHFUL. Salvation is NOT AUTOMATIC in RECEIVING it or RETAINING it. Salvation IS NOT UNCONDITIONAL.* There are personal conditions one must meet, in order to *BE* saved and *STAY* saved.

No Bible support for Calvinism! Much Bible support for the opposite of *EVERY* major doctrine of Calvinism! In light of the *indisputable Bible evidence*, does it make either common, or Bible sense, to believe John Calvin's absurdities? Since no man can serve *TWO* masters, *we must choose between Calvin's word and God's Word!*

Precious Bible Gems

In this conclusion, I want to share with you a BIBLE PRINCIPLE that will be most helpful to you in your quest for BIBLE TRUTH; as well as in the development of your understanding of BIBLE PRINCIPLES. I have discovered that *SURFACE SCANNING OF SCRIPTURE* always leads to error. *The primary doctrines of some denominations are BASED upon SHALLOW CONCEPTS derived by that very practice*—surface scanning of Scripture. But, Paul taught in 2 Timothy 2:15 that *WE MUST BE DILIGENT (STUDY)*, in order to *RIGHTLY DIVIDE* (understand and teach) God's Word. Otherwise, we fall into error; and in the end will be *ASHAMED* of our haste in building our beliefs and doctrines on unsound (unbiblical) ground.

In Bible reading, a particular word, phrase, or verse may sound like it supports the reader's personal belief; *and the process of speculation begins. If proven biblical principles are not adhered to, then error is conceived in the mind of the SPECULATOR; and that error eventually BECOMES an unchallengeable doctrine.* Denominations have been built on such *flimsy, unscriptural, manmade doctrinal foundations.* The Bible clearly teaches that in the mouth of two or three witnesses every word has to be established. *In the case of SOUND biblical doctrines, multiple witnesses agree with one another on the issue.*

The Bible follows its own *PATTERN.* Not merely two, but three of the most trusted witnesses in all Scripture practiced that principle—Moses, our Lord, and Paul. In fact, each of those three mentioned that very principle at least two times. They practiced what they preached.

In Numbers 35:30, Moses said no one should be put to death upon the testimony of just one witness *regarding crimes demanding the death-penalty*. He said the same in Deuteronomy 17:6 and 19:15.

Jesus agreed in Matthew 18:16: *"If he [the one you confronted about his sin] will not listen to you, take with you one or two more—that 'by the mouth of two or three witnesses every word may be established.'"* Read John 8:17-18 as well. (At least two times for Jesus.)

In 2 Corinthians 13:1, Paul wrote: "This will be the third time I am coming to you—By the mouth of two or three witnesses every word must be established." Also see 1 Timothy 5:19. Hebrews 10:28 duplicates that.

That same biblical principle must be honored in the formation of doctrine. Never accept anybody's theology, which is not based upon clear scriptural teaching from two or more Scripture passages. The more the better!

In Calvin's case, not only did he *BASE MANY* of his doctrines on *JUST ONE* Scripture passage, but actually founded some of them upon *NO* Scripture at all! *Calvin established questionable doctrines upon the SUPPOSED SECRET WILL OR COUNSEL of God.* He would fall back on that *PLOY* when he could find *NO* Scripture passage that clearly supported his teaching. Moreover, *the man even insinuated that some Scripture passages not only do not express God's true will, but states the opposite of His will. God's SECRET COUNSEL does not appear in Scripture, but John Calvin supposedly saw it BETWEEN Scripture lines. CALVINISM IS A CURSE,* which must be exposed and eliminated! This book is a start.

Lightning Source UK Ltd.
Milton Keynes UK
UKHW011014070223
416609UK00006B/1519